Katakana chart

h	n	d	t	z(j)	s	g	k	
ハ	ナ	ダ	タ	ザ	サ	ガ	カ	ア a
ヒ	ニ	(ヂ) ji	チ chi	ジ ji	シ shi	ギ	キ	イ i
フ	ヌ	(ヅ) zu	ツ tsu	ズ	ス	グ	ク	ウ u
ヘ	ネ	デ	テ	ゼ	セ	ゲ	ケ	エ e
ホ	ノ	ド	ト	ゾ	ソ	ゴ	コ	オ o
ヒャ hya	ニャ nya		チャ cha	ジャ ja	シャ sha	ギャ gya	キャ kya	
		ディ di	ティ ti					
ヒュ hyu	ニュ nyu		チュ chu	ジュ jyu	シュ shu	ギュ gyu	キュ kyu	
		デュ du	チェ che	ジェ je	シェ she			
ヒョ hyo	ニョ nyo		チョ cho	ジョ jo	ショ sho	ギョ gyo	キョ kyo	

Authors' acknowledgements

Special thanks are due to the following people who have made valuable contributions to the Course Book and the CDs.

Yukari Irie, Yukie Nishimura, Rie Kitamura and their families for generously providing personal photos; Hitoshi Shingai on behalf of the Tourist Section of Beppu City and Oita City for providing photos of Beppu and the monkeys of Mt Takasaki; Kyoto Studio Park for providing photos of Uzumasa Movie World; Bronwyn Dewar for advice and assistance; Masato Kobayashi for writing and recording the songs; Aki Okada, Shoko Uchikura, Tomoko Uenoyama, Yasuhito Kawabata and Yoko Masano for singing the songs; Rie Kitamura for writing the music for the song in the Teacher's Book; Gregory Parke for writing and recording the introductory music, the musical interval sound and the Momotaro music; John Rix of the recording studio Albion for patiently recording and editing the CDs; Shin Furuno, Hiroko Kikkawa, Haruo Kikkawa, Katsuhiko Kinoshita, Kaori Karino, Maiko Nakajima, Ken Tanaka and Yasuhisa Watanabe for enthusiastically rehearsing and reading the scripts for the CDs.

mirai

JAPANESE COURSE BOOK

STAGE 2

MEG EVANS

YOKO MASANO

SETSUKO TANIGUCHI

MIWA GROVES-MORIWAKI

Longman

Sydney, Melbourne, Brisbane, Perth and associated companies around the world

Pearson Education Australia Pty Limited
95 Coventry Street
South Melbourne 3205 Australia

Offices in Sydney, Brisbane and Perth, and associated companies
throughout the world.

Copyright © Meg Evans, Yoko Masano, Setsuko Taniguchi and Miwa
Groves-Moriwaki 1999
First published 1999
Reprinted 2002

All rights reserved. Except under the conditions described in the
Copyright Act 1968 of Australia and subsequent amendments, no
part of this publication may be reproduced, stored in a retrieval
system or transmitted in any form or by any means, electronic,
mechanical, photocopying, recording or otherwise, without the prior
permission of the copyright owner.

Cover and text designed by Leigh Ashforth @ watershed art
& design
Illustrated by Kate Ashforth, Paul Könye, Dimitrios Prokopis
and Boris Silvestri
Cover illustration by Dimitrios Prokopis
Set in 12pt Goudy
Produced by Pearson Education Australia Pty Limited
Printed in Hong Kong

National Library of Australia
Cataloguing-in-Publication data

Mirai: Japanese course book. Stage 2.

ISBN 0 7339 0929 9 (course book)
ISBN 0 7339 1213 3 (activity book)
ISBN 0 7339 1367 9 (teacher's book)
ISBN 0 7339 1214 1 (CDs)

1. Japanese language – Textbooks for foreign speakers –
English. 2. Japanese language – Problems, exercises, etc.
I. Evans, Meg, 1935–.

495.682421

The
publisher's
policy is to use
**paper manufactured
from sustainable forests**

Contents

LOTE National Profile Grids		x
Introduction		xv
Katakana		xix

PART 1 かっこいい かぞく
Fantastic families　Objectives ✶ ✶ ✶ ✶ ✶ ✶ ✶ ✶ ✶ ✶ 1

UNIT 1　父は スタントマンです　Dad is a stuntman ✶ ✶ ✶ ✶ ✶ ✶ ✶ 2

あきのやまに ききましょう	Let's ask Akinoyama/Particle が ✶ ✶ ✶ ✶ ✶ ✶ ✶	4
がんばれ	You can do it! Sentence patterns ✶ ✶ ✶ ✶ ✶ ✶	5
もうすこし	なんにんですか。How many people? ✶ ✶ ✶ ✶	6
もうすこし	My family and yours: comparison ✶ ✶ ✶ ✶ ✶ ✶ ✶	7
やってみよう	Let's do it: わたし／ぼくの かぞく ✶ ✶ ✶ ✶ ✶ ✶	8
やってみよう	Let's do it: かよこさんの かぞく ✶ ✶ ✶ ✶ ✶ ✶	9
日本からの Ｅメール	Email from Japan ✶ ✶ ✶ ✶ ✶ ✶ ✶ ✶ ✶ ✶ ✶ ✶	10
やってみよう	Let's do it: いろいろ ✶ ✶ ✶ ✶ ✶ ✶ ✶ ✶ ✶ ✶ ✶ ✶	11
やった！	I did it! ✶ ✶ ✶ ✶ ✶ ✶ ✶ ✶ ✶ ✶ ✶ ✶ ✶ ✶ ✶ ✶ ✶ ✶ ✶	12
カタカナ	Katakana: ロ、テ、デ、オ、ス、ズ、タ、ダ、ト、ド、マ、ン	13
カタカナ れんしゅう	Katakana practice/Kanji: 父、人 ✶ ✶ ✶ ✶ ✶ ✶	14
チェック しましょう！	Let's check! ✶ ✶ ✶ ✶ ✶ ✶ ✶ ✶ ✶ ✶ ✶ ✶ ✶ ✶	15

UNIT 2　ムービーワールドで はたらいて います　He works at Movie World ✶ ✶ ✶ ✶ 16

あきのやまに ききましょう	Let's ask Akinoyama/Particle で ✶ ✶ ✶ ✶ ✶ ✶	18
がんばれ	You can do it! Sentence patterns ✶ ✶ ✶ ✶ ✶	19
もうすこし	だれが やりましたか ✶ ✶ ✶ ✶ ✶ ✶ ✶ ✶ ✶ ✶	20
やってみよう	Let's do it: いろいろ ✶ ✶ ✶ ✶ ✶ ✶ ✶ ✶ ✶ ✶ ✶ ✶	21
日本からの Ｅメール	Email from Japan ✶ ✶ ✶ ✶ ✶ ✶ ✶ ✶ ✶ ✶ ✶ ✶	22
やってみよう	Let's do it: いろいろ ✶ ✶ ✶ ✶ ✶ ✶ ✶ ✶ ✶ ✶ ✶ ✶	24
やってみよう	Let's do it: lifestyle quiz ✶ ✶ ✶ ✶ ✶ ✶ ✶ ✶ ✶	25
やった！	I did it!/Kanji: 母、兄 ✶ ✶ ✶ ✶ ✶ ✶ ✶ ✶ ✶ ✶ ✶	26
カタカナ	Katakana: ム、ヒ、ピ、ビ、ワ、ル、ニ、ア、ハ、パ、バ、イ	27
カタカナ れんしゅう	Katakana practice ✶ ✶ ✶ ✶ ✶ ✶ ✶ ✶ ✶ ✶ ✶ ✶ ✶	28
チェック しましょう！	Let's check! ✶ ✶ ✶ ✶ ✶ ✶ ✶ ✶ ✶ ✶ ✶ ✶ ✶ ✶	29

UNIT 3	まさしくんの おばあさんは パラシュートが 好きです	Masashi's grandma likes parachuting	30
あきのやまに ききましょう		Let's ask Akinoyama/Particle から	32
がんばれ		You can do it! Sentence patterns	33
もうすこし	なにが できますか		34
もうすこし	どんな人; い and な adjectives		35
やってみよう		Let's do it: どんな ペンパルが いいですか	36
やってみよう		Let's do it: いろいろ	37
やってみよう		Let's do it: いろいろ	38
日本からの Eメール		Email from Japan	39
やった！		I did it!/Kanji: 女、子、好	41
カタカナ		Katakana: ラ、シ、ジ、ユ、フ、プ、ブ、レ、セ、ゼ、ク、グ、リ	42
カタカナ れんしゅう		Katakana practice	43
チェック しましょう！		Let's check!	44

PART 2 どうぶつも ともだち
Animals are friends too — Objectives 45

UNIT 4	まさしくんの うちは おもしろい	Masashi's house is interesting	46
あきのやまに ききましょう		Let's ask Akinoyama/Particle に	48
がんばれ		You can do it! Sentence patterns	49
もうすこし	ぼくの うちは 大きくないです		50
やってみよう		Let's do it: あまのじゃく ゲーム	51
もうすこし	しんいちくんの うち		52
やってみよう		Let's do it: いろいろ	53
もうすこし	ホームステイの うちで／これ、それ、あれ、どれ		54
やってみよう		Let's do it: いろいろ	55
日本からの Eメール		Email from Japan	56
やった！		I did it!/Kanji: 大、小	58
カタカナ		Katakana: ツ、ヘ、ペ、ベ、ケ、ゲ、サ、ザ、ナ、メ、キ、ギ、コ、ゴ	59
カタカナ れんしゅう		Katakana practice	60
チェック しましょう！		Let's check!	61

mirai 2

UNIT 5	へびも かえるが すき	Snakes like frogs too	62

あきのやまに ききましょう	Let's ask Akinoyama/Particle や	64
がんばれ	You can do it! Sentence patterns	65
もうすこし	なんびき いますか	66
もうすこし	いろいろな いろ	67
日本からの Eメール	Email from Japan	68
もうすこし	はなこは かわいい ようふくが 大好き	70
やってみよう	Let's do it: いろいろ	71
やってみよう	Let's do it: トムくんは かみが くろいです	72
やってみよう	Let's do it: なにいろの T-シャツが 好きですか	73
やった！	I did it!/Kanji: 口、目	74
カタカナ	Katakana: ミ、モ、ウ、エ、ネ、ヌ、ノ、カ、ガ	75
カタカナ れんしゅう	Katakana practice	76
チェック しましょう！	Let's check!	77

UNIT 6	あなの 中に なにが いますか	What's in the hole?	78

あきのやまに ききましょう	Let's ask Akinoyama/Particle まで	80
がんばれ	You can do it! Sentence patterns	81
もうすこし	ここ、そこ、あそこ	82
	まちへ なにをしに いきますか	82
もうすこし	あきらくんは どこに いますか	83
日本からの Eメール	Email from Japan	84
もうすこし	てを いれては だめです	86
もうすこし	おいしいです。おいしかったです	87
やってみよう	Let's do it: しゅうまつは どうでしたか	88
やってみよう	Let's do it: いろいろ	89
やってみよう	Let's do it: いろいろ	90
やった！	I did it!/Kanji: 上、下、中	91
カタカナ	Katakana: ソ、ヤ、ヨ、チ、ホ、キャ、ギャ、キュ、ギュ、キョ、ギョ	92
カタカナ れんしゅう	Katakana practice	93
チェック しましょう！	Let's check!	94

PART 3 あそびに いきましょう
Let's have fun Objectives ✶ ✶ ✶ ✶ ✶ ✶ ✶ ✶ ✶ ✶ 95

UNIT 7 スキーに いきたい   I want to go skiing ✶ ✶ ✶ ✶ ✶ ✶ 96

あきのやまに ききましょう	Let's ask Akinoyama/Particle で ✶ ✶ ✶ ✶ ✶ ✶ ✶ ✶	98
がんばれ	You can do it! Sentence patterns ✶ ✶ ✶ ✶ ✶ ✶ ✶	99
もうすこし	テニスが したいです ✶ ✶ ✶ ✶ ✶ ✶ ✶ ✶ ✶ ✶ ✶	100
やってみよう	Let's do it: いろいろ ✶ ✶ ✶ ✶ ✶ ✶ ✶ ✶ ✶ ✶ ✶ ✶	101
もうすこし	スキーは たのしくなかったです ✶ ✶ ✶ ✶ ✶ ✶	102
やってみよう	Let's do it: やすみは どうでしたか ✶ ✶ ✶ ✶ ✶	103
	Let's do it: あしたは なにを しますか ✶ ✶ ✶ ✶	103
もうすこし	Let's do it: きょうは いいてんきですね ✶ ✶ ✶ ✶	104
やってみよう	Let's do it: いろいろ ✶ ✶ ✶ ✶ ✶ ✶ ✶ ✶ ✶ ✶ ✶ ✶	105
日本からの Eメール	Email from Japan ✶ ✶ ✶ ✶ ✶ ✶ ✶ ✶ ✶ ✶ ✶ ✶ ✶	106
やった！	I did it!/Kanji: 見、山 ✶ ✶ ✶ ✶ ✶ ✶ ✶ ✶ ✶ ✶	108
カタカナ	Katakana: シャ、ジャ、シュ、ジュ、シェ、ジェ、ショ、ジョ、チャ、チュ、チェ、チョ ✶ ✶ ✶ ✶ ✶ ✶ ✶ ✶	109
カタカナ れんしゅう	Katakana practice ✶ ✶ ✶ ✶ ✶ ✶ ✶ ✶ ✶ ✶ ✶ ✶	110
チェック しましょう！	Let's check! ✶ ✶ ✶ ✶ ✶ ✶ ✶ ✶ ✶ ✶ ✶ ✶ ✶ ✶ ✶ ✶	111

UNIT 8 わさびは とても からい！   The wasabi is very hot! ✶ ✶ ✶ ✶ 112

あきのやまに ききましょう	Let's ask Akinoyama/Particle で ✶ ✶ ✶ ✶ ✶ ✶	114
がんばれ	You can do it! Sentence patterns ✶ ✶ ✶ ✶ ✶ ✶	115
もうすこし	ひとつ、いっぱい、いちまい ✶ ✶ ✶ ✶ ✶ ✶ ✶ ✶ ✶	116
もうすこし	おちゃが ほしいです／ほしくないです ✶ ✶ ✶	117
やってみよう	Let's do it: いろいろ ✶ ✶ ✶ ✶ ✶ ✶ ✶ ✶ ✶ ✶ ✶ ✶	118
やってみよう	Let's do it: いろいろ ✶ ✶ ✶ ✶ ✶ ✶ ✶ ✶ ✶ ✶ ✶ ✶	119
日本からの Eメール	Email from Japan ✶ ✶ ✶ ✶ ✶ ✶ ✶ ✶ ✶ ✶ ✶ ✶ ✶	120
やった！	I did it!/Kanji: 行、円 ✶ ✶ ✶ ✶ ✶ ✶ ✶ ✶ ✶ ✶ ✶	122
カタカナ	Katakana: ティ、ディ、デュ、ニャ、ニュ、ヒュ、ビュ、ピュ ✶	123
カタカナ れんしゅう	Katakana practice ✶ ✶ ✶ ✶ ✶ ✶ ✶ ✶ ✶ ✶ ✶ ✶	124
チェック しましょう！	Let's check! ✶ ✶ ✶ ✶ ✶ ✶ ✶ ✶ ✶ ✶ ✶ ✶ ✶ ✶ ✶	125

UNIT 9	あの あかい バッグは いくらですか	How much is that red bag? * * * 126

あきのやまに ききましょう	Let's ask Akinoyama/Particle に * * * * * 128
がんばれ	You can do it! Sentence patterns * * * * * 129
もうすこし	なん月ですか * * * * * * * * * * * * 130
もうすこし	なんにちですか * * * * * * * * * * * 131
日本からの Eメール	Email from Japan * * * * * * * * * * 132
もうすこし	いくらですか／なんかいですか * * * 134
もうすこし	かいものを しましょう * * * * * * 135
やってみよう	Let's do it: いろいろ * * * * * * * * * 136
やった！	I did it!/Kanji: 車、万 * * * * * * * * 137
カタカナ	Katakana: ファ、フィ、フェ、フォ、ミュ、リュ、ウェ、ウォ、ヴァ、ヴィ、ヴ、ヴェ、ヴォ * * * * * * * * * * * * * * 138
カタカナ れんしゅう	Katakana practice * * * * * * * * * * * 139
チェック しましょう！	Let's check! * * * * * * * * * * * * * 140

PART 4 ぶんかさい
Cultural festival Objectives * * * * * * * * 141

UNIT 10	なにを しましょうか	What shall we do? * * * * * * 142

カタカナで なまえを かきましょう！	Writing names using katakana * * * * * 143
おりがみで かえるを つくりましょう！	Making an origami frog * * * * * * * 144
うたいましょう！	Let's sing * * * * * * * * * * * * * * 145
てまきずしで パーティーを しましょう！	Temakizushi party! * * * * * * * * * 146
T-シャツに かんじを かきましょう！	Drawing kanji on T-shirts * * * * * * 147
げき: タジーそばは いちばん	Play: Tassie Soba Is the Best * * * * * 148
げき: ももたろう	Play: Momotaro (The Peach Boy) * * * 150
チェック しましょう！	Let's check! * * * * * * * * * * * * * 154

VOCABULARY

| English–Japanese * * * * * * * * * * * * 155 |
| Japanese–English * * * * * * * * * * * * 162 |

LOTE – National Profile Correlation Grids

The following grids are an interpretation of the national profiles and can be used as a course outline. The references on the grids are to page numbers in the Course Book (CB); the Activity Book (AB); and the Teacher's Book (TB). The Aesthetic strand mentioned in the national profiles is taken to mean imaginative and creative learning experiences. Suggestions for these will be found mainly in the Teacher's Book.

Units 1–2
Proposed time span: 6–7 weeks
Content: Families, counting people, working and studying, likes and dislikes

Main linguistic elements

Sentence patterns: なんにん かぞくですか。お兄さんが います(か)。兄が 一人 います。
あねは いません。　　　　　[Place]で 〜て います(か)
Katakana: ロ、テデ、オ、スズ、タダ、トド、マ、ン、ム、ヒビピ、ワ、ル、ニ、ア、ハバパ、イ
Kanji: 父、人、母、兄　(Extension: 妹、弟、何、姉)　Particles: が、で

Strands

Outcomes — Learners can:
- say how many family members they have
- understand others talking about family
- say where people work or study
- read and write a short letter
- read and write 4–8 kanji

Strand organisers: Interpersonal, Informational, Imaginative/creative, Script

Activities (multilevel strategies): もうすこし やってみよう、日本からのEメール、Summary (やった)、カタカナ、きましょう、かいわ、よみかきの れんしゅう、ことばの パズル、Extension activities、Kanji、まんが、Self-assessment

Cultural awareness:
- sumo
- Tengu, Kappa
- history of katakana
- Japanese family system
- use of polite names for family members
- work and school in Japan

Listening and speaking

Learning activities:
- matching family members to a family tree — Interpersonal ● — CB 11 — TB — CB xvii
- following a story — Informational ● — CB 24 — CB xvii
- role play — Imaginative/creative ● — AB 2, 13 — CB xiii
- identifying family members from taped material — Informational ● — CB 4, 10
- conducting a quiz — Interpersonal ● — CB 6, 20 — CB 25, 21 — CB 10, 22 — AB 1, 12 — CB 15, 29 — CB 18, 22
- playing language games — Interpersonal ●
- responding to taped material

Reading

- reading a story/dialogue — Informational ● — story/dialogue — CB 2, 18
- reading an email — Informational ● — email — CB 10, 22
- reading labelled photos — Informational ● — labelled photos — CB 8, 9
- playing games — Imaginative/creative ● — riddles — AB 6
- reading riddles — Interpersonal ● — quiz — AB 17
- reading a quiz — Script ● — manga — AB 9, 20
- reading a manga — Imaginative/creative ● — katakana — CB 13, 26 — AB 11
- completing puzzles — Script ● — kanji — CB 14, 26 — AB 5, 26
- reading a summary — Informational ● — puzzles — CB 12, 26 — AB 9, 20
- summary (やった)

Writing

- copying katakana syllables — Script ● — AB 3
- copying kanji — Script ● — AB 14
- completing sentences — Script ● — CB 10, 23 — CB 14, 28 — AB 7–8, 17–18 — AB 10–11, 21–22 — TB — AB 5, 16
- writing an email/letter — Informational ●
- preparing a family tree — Interpersonal ●
- writing a manga — Imaginative/creative ● — AB 9, 20
- completing puzzles — Script ●

mirai 2

Units 3–4
Proposed time span: 6–7 weeks

Content: Families, homes, pets, likes and dislikes, abilities

Main linguistic elements

Sentence patterns: なにが すきですか。～がすき／きらいです。～は すきじゃないです。～が すきです。でも、～は きらいです。～が できます。～は できません。[Place]から きました。へやに なにが います／ありますか。～は どこに います／ありますか。これは なんですか。い and な adjectives (positive and negative usage). これ／それ／あれ.

Katakana: ラ、シジ、ユ、プフブ、レ、セゼ、クグ、リ、ツ、ヘベペ、ケゲ、サザ、ナ、メ、キギ、コゴ m

Kanji: 女、子、好、大、小 (Extension: 名、前、男、来) Particles: から、に

Strands

Outcomes — Learners can:
- discuss likes and dislikes
- discuss abilities
- say where people, pets and objects are
- describe homes
- read and write a short letter
- read and write 5–9 more kanji

Strand organisers: Interpersonal, Informational, Imaginative/creative, Script

Activities (multilevel strategies): もうすこし やってみよう、日本からのEメール、Summary (やった)、カタカナ、きさましょう、かいわ、よみかきの れんしゅう、ことばの パズル、Extension activities、Kanji、まんが、Self-assessment

Cultural awareness:
- koinobori
- inside a Japanese home:
  - tatami
  - genkan
  - shōji
  - butsudan
  - (o)furo

Listening and speaking

Learning activities:
- selecting preferences
- choosing a suitable present
- role play
- recognising a room plan
- playing language games
- understanding a taped letter
- responding to taped material

CB 34, 53, 55; AB 23, 34; AB 24, 35; CB 37, 38, 51; TB; CB 44, 61
Cultural: CB 32, CB 52, CB 56, 57

Reading

Learning activities:
- reading a story/dialogue
- reading a labelled house
- reading an email/letter
- choosing a pen friend
- responding to written extracts
- playing games
- completing puzzles
- reading a manga

story/dialogue	CB 30, 45
choosing a penpal	CB 36
email	CB 39, 56
responding to written extracts	AB 30, 39
manga	CB 54 / AB 31, 42
katakana	CB 42 / AB 44
kanji	CB 41, 58 / AB 27, 38
word puzzles	CB 43 / AB 32, 43
playing games	TB
summary (やった)	CB 41, 58

Writing

Learning activities:
- copying katakana, kanji
- completing sentences
- writing a menu
- writing a reply
- inserting dialogue
- writing a manga
- completing puzzles

CB 37, 38, 55, 57; CB 39, 43; AB 25, 26, 27, 39, 41, 43; AB 28, 30, 32, 43; AB 27, 38, 31, 42; TB

LOTE National Profile grids — xi

Units 5–6	Proposed time span: 7–8 weeks
Content:	Counting animals, describing animals and people, describing where things are

Main linguistic elements	Sentence patterns: （この）かえるは あしが ながいです。ペットは なんびき いますか。なに いろの とりですか。コアラは きの上に います。コーラは れいぞうこの 中に あります。てをいれては だめです。こうえんへ あそびに いきます。この、その、あの。ここ、そこ、あそこ。Use of adjectives with past tense. Katakana: ミ、モ、ウ、エ、ネ、ヌ、ノ、カガ、ソ、ヤ、ヨ、チ、ホボポ、キャ、キュ、キョ、ギャ、ギュ、ギョ Kanji: 口、目、上、下、中 (Extension: 白、赤、食、飲)

Strands

Outcomes — Learners can:
- count animals
- describe animals and people
- say where things are
- reply to letters
- write captions to photos
- read and write 5–8 more kanji

Strand organisers: Interpersonal, Informational, Imaginative/creative, Script

Activities (multilevel strategies): もうすこし、やってみよう、日本からのEメール、Summary (やった)、カタカナ、ききましょう、かいわ、よみかきの れんしゅう、ことばの パズル、Extension activities、Kanji、まんが、Self-assessment

Cultural awareness:
- parks in Japan
- singing insects
- beetle culture
- Beppu onsen
- Takasakiyama
- Japanese macaques

Listening and speaking

Learning activities:
- following a story
- role play
- identifying animals from descriptions
- identifying band members
- playing language games
- responding to taped material

CB 66 70, CB 67 71 88 89 90, CB 68 84, AB 45 56, AB 46 57, TB, CB 77 94

- CB 68
- CB 69
- CB 69
- CB 85
- CB 85

Reading

Learning activities:
- reading a story/dialogue
- reading an email
- responding to written texts
- playing games
- completing puzzles
- reading a manga
- reading a quiz

story/dialogue	CB 62, 78
email	CB 68, 84
responding to a written text	CB 70, 86, 88
game	TB
quiz	CB 73, 83
manga	CB 82 AB 53, 64
katakana	CB 75, 93 AB 66
kanji	CB 74, 91 AB 49, 60
word puzzles	CB 66 AB 54, 65
summary (やった)	CB 74, 91

Writing

Learning activities:
- copying katakana, kanji
- completing sentences
- writing replies
- inserting dialogue
- completing puzzles
- describing own room
- writing captions
- writing a manga

CB 68 84, CB 75 93 AB 47 58, AB 50 52 61 63, AB 65 76, TB, AB 49 60

xii   mirai 2

Units 7–8	Proposed time span: 7–8 weeks
Content:	Leisure, eating out, weather, desires

Main linguistic elements	Sentence patterns: どこへ いきたいですか。えいがを みにいきたくないです。日本ごで はなしましょう。おはしで たべましょう。やきとりを 一つください。おちゃが ほしいです。コーラは ほしくないです。ラジオで ききました。おいしそうです。ゆきが ふっています。Past negative use of adjectives. Counters: 〜つ、〜まい、〜はい。 Katakana: シャ、ジャ、シュ、ジュ、シェ、ジェ、ショ、ジョ、チャ、チュ、チョ、チェ、ティ、ディ、デュ、ニャ、ニュ、ニョ Kanji: 見、山、行、円 (Extension: 海、町、高、安) Particle: で

Outcomes

Learners can:
- say where they want to/don't want to go
- describe the weather
- order a meal
- say what they want/don't want
- read and write passages in *kanamajiri*

Strand organisers: Interpersonal, Informational, Imaginative/creative, Script

Activities (multilevel strategies): もうすこし、やってみよう、日本からの E メール、Summary (やった)、カタカナ、ききましょう、かいわ、よみかきの れんしゅう、ことばの パズル、Extension activities、Kanji、まんが、Self-assessment

Cultural awareness
- historic Kurashiki
- restaurants
- Japanese food
  kaitenzushi
  sobaya
- use of the honorific お
- use of お〜やさん

Listening and speaking

Learning activities:
- following a story
- role play
- understanding a weather forecast
- understanding a food order
- playing language games
- responding to taped material

Activities refs: CB 67 78, CB 101 103 104 117 118 119, CB 106 120, AB 68 79, TB, CB 111 125, • CB 106–7, • CB 120–1

Reading

- reading a story/dialogue — story/dialogue CB 96, 112
- reading an email — email CB 106, 120
- responding to written messages — responding to messages AB 72
- playing games — manga AB 75, 86
- completing puzzles — katakana CB 110, 124
- reading a manga — kanji CB 108, 122
- word puzzles AB 76, 87
- summary (やった) CB 108, 122

Writing

- copying katakana, kanji
- completing sentences
- answering questions
- completing puzzles
- inserting dialogue
- writing a reply
- labelling photos
- writing a food order
- completing puzzles

Refs: CB 106 120, AB 69 70 80 81 88, CB 124 110, AB 73 74 83, AB 87 76, AB 71 82

LOTE National Profile grids

Units 9–10
Content: Shopping, dates, bunkasai
Proposed time span: 6–7 weeks

Main linguistic elements	Sentence patterns: きょう（きのう）は なん月 なん日です（でした）か。 [Person]に 〜を かいます。 〜は いくらですか。〜のうりばは どこですか。 Months; days of the month; dates; numbers up to 100,000. Katakana: ファ、フィ、フェ、フォ、ミュ、リュ、ウェ、ウォ、ヴァ、ヴィ、ヴ、ヴェ、ヴォ Kanji: 車、万 (Extension: 百、千)　　　　　　　Particle: に

Strands

Outcomes — Learners can:
- go shopping
- understand dates
- follow written instructions
- take part in or read a play
- read and write passages in *kanamajiri*

Strand organisers: Interpersonal, Informational, Imaginative/creative, Script

Activities (multilevel strategies): もうすこしやってみよう、日本からのEメール、Summary (やった)、カタカナ、ききましょう、かいわ、よみかきの れんしゅう、ことばの パズル、Extension activities、Kanji、まんが、Self-assessment

Cultural awareness:
- days of the month
- counting floors
- seasons
- department store greetings
- Uzumasa Movie World
- Momotaro

Listening and speaking

Learning activities:
- following a story ● (Interpersonal) — CB 134, 135, 136 — CB 128
- role play ● — CB 132
- responding to information ● — CB 133
- listening for information ● — AB 90, AB 145, 148, 150 — CB 150
- singing songs ● (Imaginative/creative)
- taking part in a play ●
- playing language games ●
- responding to taped material ● — AB 89 — CB 140, 154

Reading

Learning activities:
- reading a story/dialogue ● — story/dialogue CB 126–7
- reading an email ● — email CB 132–3
- following written directions ● — following directions CB 146–7
- reading a play ● — reading a play CB 148, 150
- completing puzzles ● — reading dialogues CB 135
- responding to writing ● — manga AB 97
- reading dialogues ● — katakana CB 138, 144 AB 91
- reading a manga ● — kanji CB 137 AB 93
- word puzzles AB 98
- summary (やった) CB 137

Writing

Learning activities:
- copying katakana, kanji ● (Script) — AB 91
- completing sentences ● — AB 92
- inserting dialogue ● — AB 99
- answering questions ● — CB 132 — AB 99 — AB 94 — TB
- writing a manga ● — CB 139
- completing puzzles ● — AB 95
- writing a letter ● — 144 — 96

xiv　　　mirai 2

Introduction

こんにちは！
Welcome to Mirai Stage 2.

With the aid of the materials in *Mirai Stage 2* and the help of your teacher you should soon be able to communicate with Japanese people about your family, friends, house, pets and other animals, and your leisure activities. You will also learn the entire katakana syllabary, quite a few more kanji and a lot more about Japan.

In Unit 10 you will find a number of activities that will help your class to stage a successful language and culture event.

Apart from Hiro, who had to return to Japan, the judo academy characters that you met in *Mirai Stage 1* are still good friends. They still attend the judo academy and they spend much of their leisure time together. You'll be reading about some of the things they got up to this year as you go through the book.

- Tanaka-sensei
- Karen Scott
- Johnny Lee
- Naomi Akimoto
- Ken Thomson
- Masashi Yamada
- Nicki Fenwick

Katakana and kanji

You will learn eight katakana in each unit in *Mirai Stage 2*. Since katakana is used for foreign words and phrases, you will be able to write lots of words immediately with the katakana syllables you are learning. Now that you can read hiragana, roomaji will occur only under words containing new katakana syllables.

You will also learn two or three kanji per unit. We know that some of you love learning kanji and want to be able to read more than this, so we have presented more kanji in the *Stage 2 Activity Book* in a section called 'Kanji Kings'.

Spacing

Although Japanese writing normally does not have spaces between words, in *Mirai Stage 1* we placed a space between every word to help you learn to read. In *Mirai Stage 2* we have removed the space between です, or variations of です, and the word that comes before it. This is to help you gradually become used to reading sentences without spaces.

We have chosen a grand champion sumo, Akinoyama, and his friends to help you through *Mirai Stage 2*.

Sumō is the national sport of Japan and is at least 1500 years old. Japan is a highly developed, modern country with a fascinating culture. In the sport of sumō part of the ancient culture of Japan is preserved. Those who watch the sport enjoy the skill of the wrestlers but also love seeing the ancient traditions still performed.

Japanese people have learned to live with many natural disasters — earthquakes, typhoons, mud slides and huge falls of snow are not uncommon. Understandably, many people prayed to the gods for delivery from these disasters as well as for good harvests. Centuries ago, sumō bouts were performed within the precincts of the shrines, together with sacred dancing and drama, to ask the gods for favourable treatment.

In the 8th century the emperor established his court at Nara, making it the nation's first capital. Sumō wrestling bouts soon became an established feature of life at the imperial court, and formal rules and techniques evolved that have changed little since then. Champion wrestlers such as Akinoyama, your helper, are admired throughout Japan for their:

✧ great skill   ✧ dignity   ✧ determination

Sumō tournaments are preceded by a ceremony in which the teams take turns to enter the ring in reverse order of their rank. Each wrestler wears a very costly ceremonial apron made of richly embroidered silk hemmed with a gold fringe.

The *yokozuna* (the grand champion) plays the leading role in the ceremony. He claps his hands to attract the attention of the gods, puts his hands face upwards to show he conceals no weapons and, raising his legs high in the air one after the other, he brings them down with a loud thump to drive all evil from the ring.

The *gyōji* (referees) wear kimonos patterned after the style of 16th-century samurai. *Gyōji* are also ranked; only top *gyōji* can referee a bout between champions. The rank of the *gyōji* can be seen from the colour of the tassel on his fan, purple or purple and white being reserved for the highest-ranking *gyōji*.

There are many throws used in sumō. The challenge is to lift your opponent out of the ring or to make any part of your opponent's body apart from his feet touch the floor. It's very exciting to see a smaller sumō throw a much larger sumō out of the ring by using superior skills and tactics.

Finding your way around this Course Book

The first section, called 'Katakana', is a detailed explanation of the katakana syllabary. In this Course Book you will learn how to read and write katakana. You should read this section before you start so you have some understanding of what katakana is used for.

The rest of the book is divided into four parts. The first three parts each have three units; the fourth part contains plays, songs, recipes and activities you could use for a LOTE evening. Within the nine study units the following icons tell you what to expect.

On the opening page of each part the *gyōji* will show what you will be able to do after you have completed three units.

This indicates that the section is on compact disc (CD).

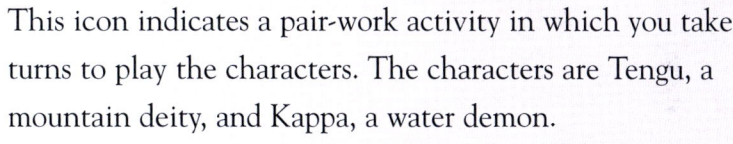

This icon indicates a pair-work activity in which you take turns to play the characters. The characters are Tengu, a mountain deity, and Kappa, a water demon.

Tengu is a deity who is said to inhabit mountains. In ancient Japan, Tengu was thought to have supernatural powers. It is part bird and part human. It is distinguished by an enormous nose and often wears a small, square hat. It has big wings with which it flies like a huge bird. There are many tales of its sword skills. It is a mischievous deity and loves to play tricks on people.

Kappa is a water demon, famous as much for tricking people as for helping them. It has an indentation on the top of its head which holds water. If Kappa spills the water it loses its magic powers. Kappa is said to be very polite, so if a human speaks politely to Kappa, Kappa must bow back and so spill the water.

あきのやまに ききましょう	In this section sumō wrestler Akinoyama will explain how to express yourself in colloquial Japanese.
が Particles	At the bottom of the page Akinoyama introduces you to new particles.
がんばれ！	Here, key sentence patterns are laid out clearly for your reference.
もう すこし	Here you will find extra vocabulary and expressions to extend the range of what you can say.
やってみよう	Try out these activities to test your understanding.
やった！	I did it! A summary to show what you know.
日本からの Eメール	Find out what Yukari and Shingo are up to as they send us email about their lives in Japan.
カタカナ	Here's where you practise reading and writing katakana.
チェック しましょう	Let's check! A vocabulary and checklist, where you can check everything you have learned and how many units you have completed. The bowls are filling up with *chanko-nabe*, which is a special high-energy stew for sumō wrestlers. It's made of different meats, fish and vegetables, cooked together in a heat-proof pot called a *nabe*.

Katakana

By now you must have seen some katakana words, such as people's names and some food. In *Mirai Stage 2* you will learn all forty-six basic katakana symbols, just as you learned the hiragana symbols in *Mirai Stage 1*. You will then be able to read and write words in katakana! Along the way, you'll be learning some new words. Often, though, you'll be learning how Japanese people pronounce words you already know!

What is katakana?

Katakana is one of the two sets of Japanese syllabic writing called *kana*, the other one being hiragana, and literally means a part- or side-script. You will notice it has sharper corners and straighter lines than hiragana.

While hiragana are actually simplified versions of selected kanji, katakana are segments extracted from whole kanji. Take the five vowel sounds, for example:

Hiragana

a	安	→	あ	→	あ	
i	以	→	い	→	い	
u	宇	→	う	→	う	
e	衣	→	え	→	え	
o	於	→	お	→	お	

Katakana

a	阿	→	ア	→	ア	
i	伊	→	イ	→	イ	
u	宇	→	ウ	→	ウ	
e	江	→	エ	→	エ	
o	於	→	オ	→	オ	

It is said that katakana were invented at the end of the Nara period, when various elements of kanji, the Chinese characters, were employed as phonetic symbols to aid Buddhist priests in reciting texts written in Chinese.

What is katakana used for in modern Japan?

Katakana is now used for writing the many words that have been adopted from other languages, including the names of places (countries, cities, towns, etc.) and people. These are just a few examples:

サッカー	sakkaa	ピクニック	pikunikku	オーストラリア	Oosutoraria
アメリカ	Amerika	シドニー	Shidonii	ワシントン	Washinton
シャロン	Sharon	スミス	Sumisu	パーカー	Paakaa
ジョン	Jon	ブラウン	Buraun	ブリスベン	Burisuben

introduction

Katakana is also used to describe all sorts of sounds around us, like the sounds animals make or the sound of a door slamming shut. Here are two examples:

Many Japanese companies are choosing to use katakana for their company names and their products. Although these companies are Japanese, the use of katakana gives them a more international image. Have you seen any of these?

| トヨタ Toyota | ニッサン Nissan | セイコー Seiko | カワサキ Kawasaki |

Recently, more and more words have been taken directly from English and given a Japanese pronunciation. Can you guess what the following words are?

| ガイドライン gaidorain | シミュレーション shimyureeshon | ポリシー porishii |

By the way, some words adopted by the Japanese have been shortened. Can you guess what these words are?

| パソコン pasokon | ファミコン famikon | リモコン rimokon |
| マスコミ masukomi | リストラ risutora | サントラ santora |

You also see many signs, shop advertisements and restaurant menus written in katakana.

The katakana syllabary

Here are the forty-six basic katakana symbols. Roomaji has been placed underneath to help you. The pronunciation of each of them is exactly the same as its hiragana counterpart.

Start here and read down.

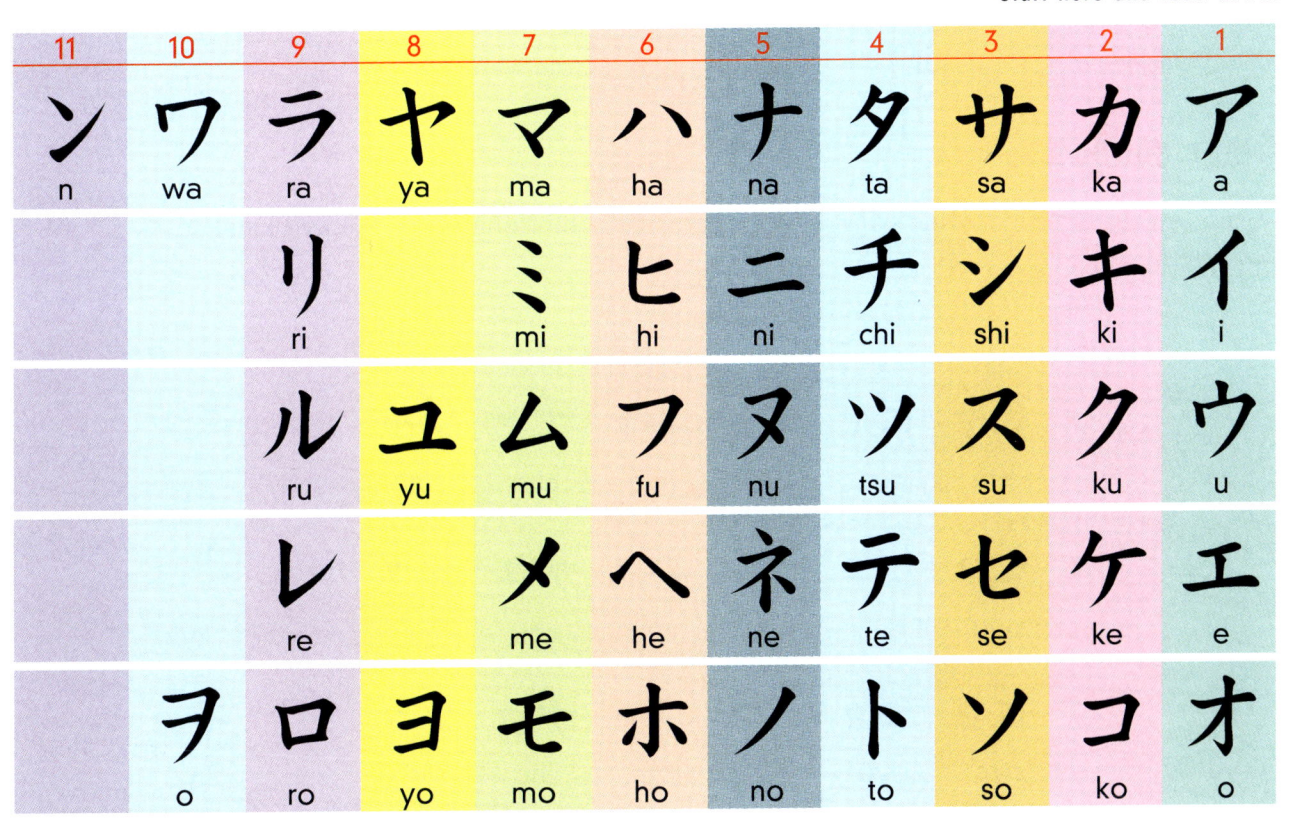

11	10	9	8	7	6	5	4	3	2	1
ン n	ワ wa	ラ ra	ヤ ya	マ ma	ハ ha	ナ na	タ ta	サ sa	カ ka	ア a
		リ ri		ミ mi	ヒ hi	ニ ni	チ chi	シ shi	キ ki	イ i
		ル ru	ユ yu	ム mu	フ fu	ヌ nu	ツ tsu	ス su	ク ku	ウ u
		レ re		メ me	ヘ he	ネ ne	テ te	セ se	ケ ke	エ e
	ヲ o	ロ ro	ヨ yo	モ mo	ホ ho	ノ no	ト to	ソ so	コ ko	オ o

By the way, ヲ (the equivalent of hiragana を) is hardly ever used, except when you write whole sentences in katakana as you would, for example, in a telegram.

introduction

Dakuten (ﾞ) and handakuten (ﾟ)

Just as with hiragana, katakana's forty-six symbols are extended by the use of two signs: **dakuten** (ﾞ) and **handakuten** (ﾟ). Syllables that start with g, z, j, d, b and p are written by putting these special little marks to the top right of the sounds that start with k, s, t and h. (Remember, you learned to do this with hiragana!) Here are a few examples of how they are used:

6	5	4	3	2	1
パ pa	バ ba	ダ da	ザ za		ガ ga
ピ pi	ビ bi	(ヂ) ji	ジ ji		ギ gi
プ pu	ブ bu	ヅ zu	ズ zu		グ gu
ペ pe	ベ be	デ de	ゼ ze		ゲ ge
ポ po	ボ bo	ド do	ゾ zo		ゴ go

Other sounds

Again as with hiragana, some syllables are created by combining a normal-sized katakana with one of three small katakana: ヤ ya, ユ yu or ヨ yo.

9		7		6		5		4		3		2	
リャ rya	ミャ mya	ピャ pya	ビャ bya	ヒャ hya	ニャ nya	チャ cha	ジャ ja	シャ sha	キャ kya
リュ ryu	ミュ myu	ピュ pyu	ビュ byu	ヒュ hyu	ニュ nyu	チュ chu	ジュ ju	シュ shu	キュ kyu
リョ ryo	ミョ myo	ピョ pyo	ビョ byo	ヒョ hyo	ニョ nyo	チョ cho	ジョ jo	ショ sho	キョ kyo

Besides the ones shown in the table there are the following:
イェ(ye), ウィ(wi), ウェ(we), ウォ(wo), シェ(she), ジェ(je), チェ(che), ティ(ti), ディ(di), デュ(du), ファ(fa), フェ(fe), フィ(fi) and フォ(fo).

By the way, when the combined syllables are written down the page, the small syllable is placed below and to the right. Compare these examples:

Long vowel sounds in katakana

A dash is used to lengthen any vowel. It is written horizontally when writing horizontally and vertically when writing vertically. It's that simple! Look at these examples:

Doubling consonants

As with hiragana, just add a little ツ (tsu), like this:

| チップス chippusu | ロケット roketto | クッキー kukkii | ココナッツ kokonattsu |

The use of ヴァ, ヴィ, ヴ, ヴェ, ヴォ

For va, vi, vu, ve and vo, both バ, ビ, ブ, ベ, ボ and ヴァ, ヴィ, ヴ, ヴェ, ヴォ are correct, but the Japanese government advises that it is preferable to use the latter so that different pronunciations are made clear. So, from today, let's try to use them!

Very commonly used words, such as テレビ (terebi) and ビデオ (bideo), are still written with バビブベボ.

introduction xxiii

Writing western names

When writing the full name of someone in katakana it is usual to place a dot between the given name and the surname. For example: トム・ジョーンズ (Tom Jones).

Tips on reading katakana

Say the word to yourself with all the vowel sounds, then try taking some of them out.
Words such as アメリカ (Amerika) are easy to read, because there is a vowel sound between each consonant in English too. Recognising other words is not as easy. For example, the word フルーツ (furuutsu) is not immediately recognisable as 'fruits' until you run the 'f' and 'r' sounds together.

How 'fruits' becomes 'furuutsu'

Japanese pronunciation requires a syllable for every sound except 'n', so 'Tom' is said 'Tomu' and 'Jones' is said 'Joonzu'. Fruits becomes 'furuutsu'. English is full of double and even triple consonants. In Japanese there is a vowel between each one.

How 'flute' becomes 'furuuto'

There are no 'l' sounds in Japanese, so English words that contain 'l' sounds are written with *ra ri ru re ro* sounds. These sounds are pronounced halfway between English *ra ri ru re ro* and *la li lu le lo*. Can you work out what this word is? オリンピック (orinpikku)

Try replacing 'ra', 'ri', 'ru', 're' and 'ro' sounds with 'la', 'li', 'lu', 'le' and 'lo'.
The word フルート (furuuto) looks like fruit until you try saying it with an 'l' sound, when it becomes 'fuluuto'. Remove the first 'u' and the last 'o' and now you can hear it says flute.

You can look back at this page if you need help.

part 1

Fantastic families

At the end of Part 1 you will be able to talk and write about:

- family members and other people's family members
- family occupations
- likes and dislikes
- abilities.

You will also find out more about Japanese families and learn some kanji and katakana.

かっこいいかぞく

Unit 1

父は スタントマンです
ちち　　　sutantoman

1. あにの ジムです。 / こんにちは。

2. Have fun. / じゃ、また。

3. かぞくは なん人ですか。 / 5人です。まさしくんは？

4. 4人です。 / きょうだいは？ / あねが 一人 います。なおみさんは？

5. わたしは 一人っこです。かぞくは 3人です。でも、父は 日本に すんで います。 / おかあさんは 日本ごの せんせいですね。 / はい、そうです。だから、わたしたちは オーストラリアに すんで います。

mirai 2

6
あ、ロデオが はじまりますよ。(rodeo)
みて ください。あにです。
おにいさんは すごいですね。
かっこいい！

7
さあ、こどもの ロデオです。
のりましょうか。
Kid's Rodeo
ぼくは うしは ちょっと...

8
わたし、のります！
え？ だいじょうぶ？
きを つけて。

9
なおみさん、かっこいい！
すごい！
きゃあ！
わたしの 父は スタントマンです。

やってみよう
さがして ください

Please look for:
* two words that mean brother
* the word for father
* how to ask *How many in the family?*
* the word for *brothers and sisters*
* where Naomi's father lives
* two words expressing admiration.

part 1 • unit 1

あきのやまに ききましょう
Let's ask Akinoyama

Why are there two ways of saying the words for family members?

In Japan we prefer to be modest about ourselves and our family, so we use words that have a humble tone for our own family members. For other people's family members we use words that have a respectful tone.

What about when you talk to your mother or father?

In this case, we use respectful language. We show our respect for our parents and older brothers and sisters by using their correct titles when we speak to them. We address our younger brothers and sisters by their name plus さん、くん or ちゃん. ちゃん is an affectionate title, something like 'dear little'. Most of us prefer to use ちゃん.

What happens if you have a stepfather or -mother or stepbrothers and -sisters. How do you talk about and to them?

In such a situation we use the same two sets of words. There *are* words for step-members of the family but we don't use them in ordinary conversation. When addressing step-members of the family we use the same respectful titles. It doesn't matter if the family member is a blood relative or not. If you go to Japan and stay with a Japanese family, you too will call the mother おかあさん and the father おとうさん. You will call any older brothers and sisters おにいさん and おねえさん and the younger children will call you by one of these titles. You can also use the children's names, but remember to add さん、くん or ちゃん.

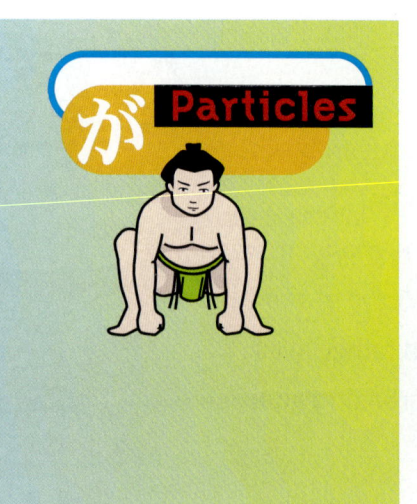

が Particles

The particle が comes after words for family members in sentences such as、あに が います. It shifts the emphasis from the topic to the subject. If you don't have a particular family member, you don't emphasise them and the particle which follows is は not が.
For example: あに<u>が</u> います。あね<u>は</u> いません。

Topic: talking about me　　Subject: It's a brother　　I have

[○] は [○] が います。

mirai 2

がんばれ

The underlined words can change.

Asking how many in the family

なんにん かぞくですか。
かぞくは なんにんですか。   or

Answer includes the speaker

ふたりです。　　　4(よ)にんです。
3にんです。　　　 5にんです。

Asking what siblings there are in the family

なんにん きょうだいですか。
きょうだいは なんにんですか。   or

Answer includes the speaker

ひとりです。　　　4にんです。
ふたりです。　　　5にんです。
3にんです。

Saying how many brothers and sisters you have

わたしは あにが ひとりと あねが ふたり います。
ぼくは おとうとが 3にんと いもうとが 4にん います。

Asking if someone has particular family members

おにいさんが いますか。　　おとうとさんが いますか。
おねえさんが いますか。　　いもうとさんが いますか。

Answering yes

はい、あにが います。
はい、あねが います。
はい、おとうとが います。
はい、いもうとが います。

Answering no

いいえ、あには いません。
いいえ、あねは いません。
いいえ、おとうとは いません。
いいえ、いもうとは いません。

Saying what brothers and sisters someone has

あきらくんは おにいさんが ひとりと おねえさんが ふたり います。
おとうとさんと いもうとさんは いません。

part 1 • unit 1

なん人ですか
How many people?

一人（1人）ひとり	二人（2人）ふたり
三人（3人）さんにん	四人（4人）よにん
五人（5人）ごにん	六人（6人）ろくにん
七人（7人）しちにん	八人（8人）はちにん
九人（9人）きゅうにん	十人（10人）じゅうにん

もうすこし！

しつもん

Using the pictures to help you, answer the questions you hear.

mirai 2

かぞく

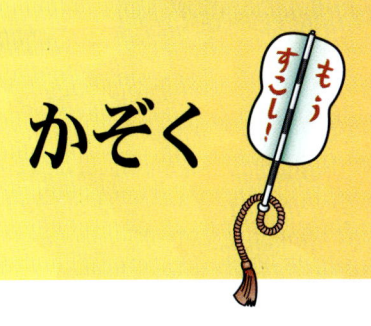

Modest words for your own family

My family

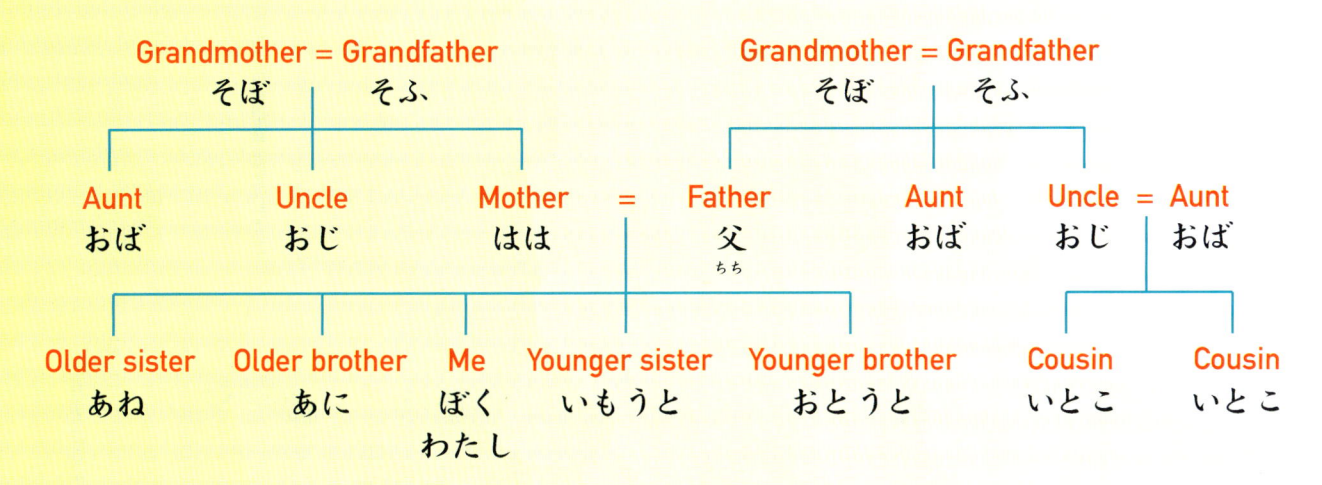

Grandmother = Grandfather					Grandmother = Grandfather			
そぼ　　　そふ					そぼ　　　そふ			

Aunt	Uncle	Mother	=	Father	Aunt	Uncle	=	Aunt
おば	おじ	はは		父 (ちち)	おば	おじ		おば

Older sister	Older brother	Me	Younger sister	Younger brother	Cousin	Cousin
あね	あに	ぼく / わたし	いもうと	おとうと	いとこ	いとこ

Polite words for others' families and for addressing your own family

Tomoko's family

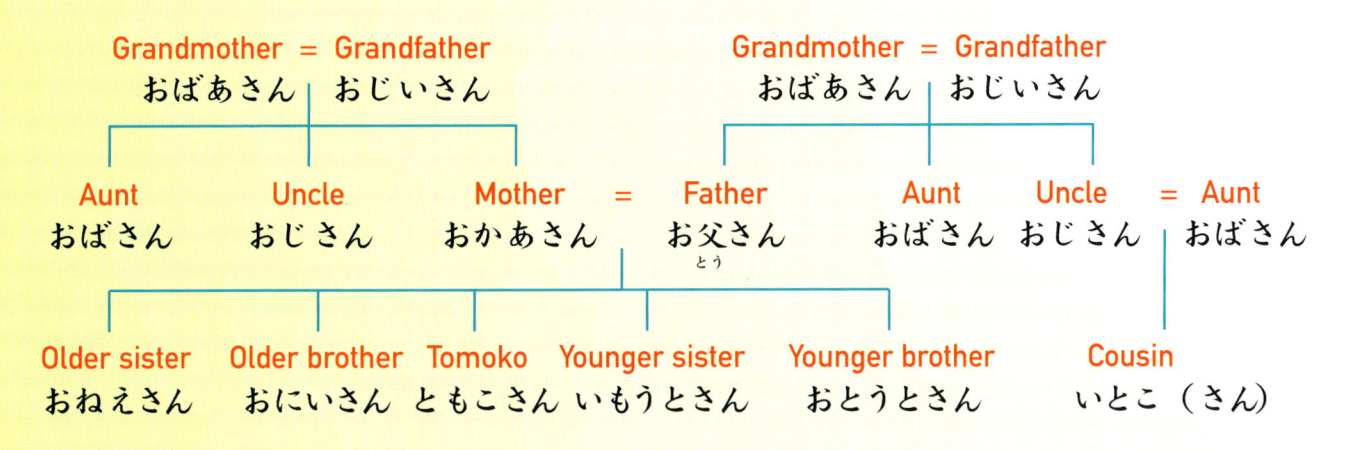

Grandmother = Grandfather					Grandmother = Grandfather			
おばあさん　おじいさん					おばあさん　おじいさん			

Aunt	Uncle	Mother	=	Father	Aunt	Uncle	=	Aunt
おばさん	おじさん	おかあさん		お父さん (とう)	おばさん	おじさん		おばさん

Older sister	Older brother	Tomoko	Younger sister	Younger brother	Cousin
おねえさん	おにいさん	ともこさん	いもうとさん	おとうとさん	いとこ（さん）

Note: When addressing either your own or other families' younger brothers, sisters and cousins, use their names (not their titles).

part 1 • unit 1

やってみよう
LET'S DO IT!

わたし／ぼくの かぞく

そふ (82)　そぼ (78)

おば (42)　おじ (45)　いとこ (15)

はは (41)　父(ちち) (44)

あね (18)
(まりこ)

あね (16)
(みき)

あに (15)
(じゅん)

ぼく (13)
(つばさ)

いもうと (8)
(えみ)

おとうと (4)
(ひろし)

パズル

1　つばさくんの かぞくは なん人ですか。
2　つばさくんは おねえさんが なん人 いますか。
3　つばさくんは おとうとさんが なん人 いますか。
4　つばさくんは きょうだいが なん人 いますか。
5　えみさんは おにいさんが なん人 いますか。
6　じゅんくんは おとうとさんが なん人 いますか。

かよこさんの かぞく

おばあさん　　　　おじいさん
(うえだ けいこ)　(うえだ たろう)

おばあさん　　　　おじいさん
(いけだ はなこ)　(いけだ けん)

おばさん　　　　おじさん　　　いとこ
(うえだ ちえ)　(うえだ たく)　(みわ)

おかあさん　　　お父さん
(いけだ ようこ)　(いけだ よしお)

おねえさん　　おにいさん　　かよこさん　　おとうとさん　　いもうとさん
(ゆき)　　　　(あきら)　　　　　　　　　　(しんご)　　　　(かおり)

パズル

1　かよこさんの おかあさんの なまえは なんですか。
2　いけだ よしおさんの お父さんは だれですか。
3　しんごくんは かよこさんの おにいさんですか。
4　ゆきさんの おじさんは だれですか。
5　あきらくんの いもうとさんは だれですか。
6　みわさんの おばあさんは だれですか。
7　かおりさんの おねえさんは だれですか。

part 1 ◆ unit 1

日本からの Eメール
Email from Japan

こんにちは。おげんきですか。かぞくは なん人ですか。わたしの かぞくは 6人です。父と ははと おとうとが 一人 います。いもうとは いません。そふと そぼも いっしょに すんで います。父は 42さいです。ははは 40さいです。そふは 70さいです。そぼは? そぼは わかりません。おとうとは 11さいです。わたしは 14さいです。さようなら。

ゆかり

Hi! Can you read my first email message to you in Japanese? **おげんきですか**, just means *Are you well?* We usually say this in letters. We don't usually say it when we meet each other as you do. Here is a photo of my grandparents. As you can see they are both very **げんき**.

Someone asked me what to say if they have family members who do not live with them. I think when we ask **かぞくは なん人ですか**, we only expect you to say who lives in the family unit in your home.

そふと そぼと わたし

There is no need to go into details about other family members. That is why I say that there are six in my family and include my grandparents who live with us. I have other grandparents who don't live with us, as well as uncles, aunts and cousins. By the way, did you notice that we have different words for older and younger brothers and sisters? Can you guess why? Tell your teacher your guess. Here is a photo of my parents, my brother and me.

父と ははと おとうとと わたし

やってみよう

Write a reply to Yukari in Japanese.

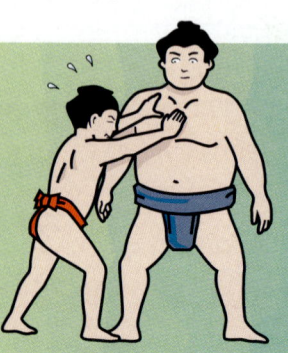

やってみよう

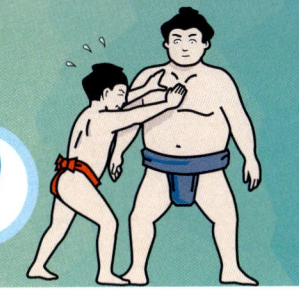

1. Mamoru, Seiko, Isamu, Rie and Miki are telling each other about their families. Listen to the conversation and find out who belongs to which family tree. Write their name and the letter of the correct family tree in your notebook. In the family trees, the white circle is the speaker. If you hear someone's age mentioned, write the person's name and age in your notebook. According to what you hear, label the circles B (boy) or G (girl).

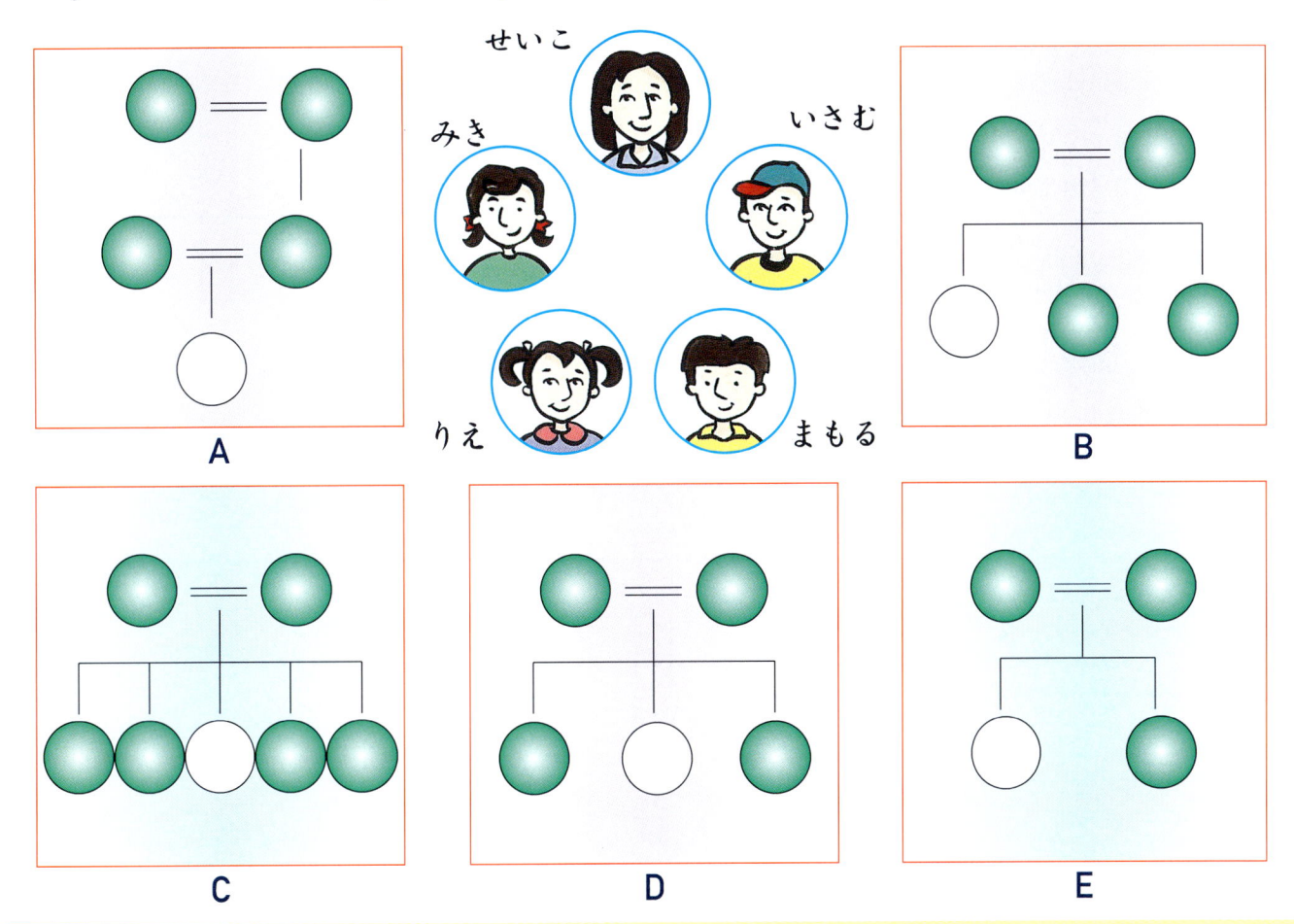

せいこ
みき
いさむ
りえ
まもる

A   B   C   D   E

2. Tengu starts. Secretly choose to be one of the five students in the above drawings. Write down your assumed name in your notebook. Kappa must find out who you are by asking questions about the family.

For example:
なん人 かぞくですか。
お父さんは なんさいですか。
When Kappa has guessed correctly, reverse roles and play again.

3. This time, Kappa can choose to be any of the children in any of the families. Write down in your notebook who you are before you start the game; for example, Rie's younger sister. This time, Tengu can ask any question *except* なん人 かぞくですか。Again, reverse roles and play again once Tengu has found out your identity.

part 1　unit 1　　11

やった！

Asking how many in the family	なん人 かぞく	は	かぞく なん人	ですか。 ですか。	or
Answering	[number] 人			です。	
Asking how many brothers and sisters	なん人 きょうだい	は	きょうだい なん人	ですか。 ですか。	or
Answering *I'm an only child*	ひとりっこ			です。	
Two (of us)	ふたり			です。	
Three (of us) or more	[number] 人			です。	

Saying how many brothers and sisters you have	わたし or ぼく	は	あに あね おとうと いもうと	が	1人 2人 3人 4人	います。
Saying how many brothers and sisters someone else has	〜さん or 〜くん		おにいさん おねえさん おとうとさん いもうとさん			
Asking if someone has a particular brother or sister			おにいさん おねえさん おとうとさん いもうとさん	が		いますか。
Answering that you have a particular brother or sister	はい、		あに あね おとうと いもうと	が		います。
Answering that you do not have a brother/sister	いいえ、		あに あね おとうと いもうと	は		いません。

カタカナ　Katakana

ロ ro	テ te / デ de	オ o	ス su / ズ zu
ロ for robot	テ for terrier	オ for oak	ス for skating
タ ta / ダ da	ト to / ド do	マ ma	ン n
タ for tadpole	ト for tongs	マ for marigold	ン for nn … good!

(ン)	ワ	ラ	ヤ	(マ)	ハ	ナ	(タ)	サ	カ	ア
	リ			ミ	ヒ	ニ	チ	シ	キ	イ
	ル		ユ	ム	フ	ヌ	ツ	(ス)	ク	ウ
	レ			メ	ヘ	ネ	(テ)	セ	ケ	エ
(ロ)		ヨ	モ	ホ	ノ	(ト)	ソ	コ	(オ)

part 1 • unit 1

カタカナ　れんしゅう

1 Can you find the names of these people in the puzzle?

スタン　デズ　ロン　トーマス　スー　ドン
Stan　Des　Ron　Thomas　Sue　Don

ス	ト	ー	マ	ス
タ	デ	ド	ロ	ン
ン	ズ	ン	ス	ー

2 Which cities are these? Choose your answer from the list.
- ローマ
- ロンドン

　a　Sydney
　b　New York
　c　London
　d　Paris
　e　Rome

漢字　かんじ

Kanji are representations of things or ideas, not sounds. Originally many kanji were pictures of the things they represent. More complex ideas were represented by combinations of kanji. Most kanji have more than one reading.

One way of remembering

父　<u>ちち</u>
　お<u>とう</u>さん
　father

Fathers sit with crossed legs in Japan. Mothers never do.

人　<u>にん</u>
　<u>じん</u>
　ひと<u>り</u>、ふた<u>り</u>
　person

A person has two legs. When this kanji occurs on the side or the top of a character, it changes shape.

On the side it looks like this: イ.

14　　　mirai 2

チェック しましょう！

My family	
あに	my older brother
あね	my older sister
いもうと	my younger sister
おとうと	my younger brother
父（ちち）	my father
そふ	my grandfather
そぼ	my grandmother
はは	my mother

Your family	
いもうとさん	younger sister
おかあさん	mother
お父さん（おとうさん）	father
おとうとさん	younger brother
おにいさん	older brother
おねえさん	older sister

Family	
かぞく	family
きょうだい	brothers and sisters
こども	child
こどもたち	children
ひとりっこ	only child

Expressions	
きをつけて	Take care
だいじょうぶ	It's okay

Question words	
なん人	how many people

Verbs	
います	has/have, there is/are
いません	hasn't/haven't, there isn't/aren't
のります	ride
のりましょう	Let's ride!
わかりません	I don't understand/know

Adjectives	
かっこいい	fantastic, cool, good-looking
げんき（な）	well

Events	
ロデオ	rodeo

Occupations	
スタントマン	stuntman

Animal	
うし	cow, bull, bullock

I can:
- ○ count people
- ○ say how many are in my family
- ○ say how many brothers and sisters I have
- ○ ask how many there are in other people's families
- ○ ask how many brothers and sisters my friends have
- ○ read and write a short letter about families
- ○ read and write 父 and 人.

part 1 • unit 1

Unit 2

ムービーワールドで はたらいて います
Muubiiwaarudo

1
- なにを して いますか。
- しゃしんを みて います。兄の ピーターです。 *(あに / piitaa)*
- みせて ください。
- どうぞ。

2
- ええっ！！バッグスバニー？？ *(Bagusubanii)* お兄さんは えいが スターですか。 *(にい)*
- いいえ、兄は ムービーワールドで *(muubiiwaarudo)* はたらいて います。

3
- お兄さんの しごとは おもしろいですね。 *(にい)*
- そうですね。

16　　　mirai 2

4 兄は 日よう日に ムービーワールドで アルバイト して います。それから 月よう日と、火よう日と、水よう日に、だいがくで べんきょうして います。

5 お兄さんは なにを べんきょうして いますか。

もちろん、えいがの ぎじゅつを べんきょうして います。

6 まさしくんも、ギターを ならって いますね。

ええ。

7 いっしょに れんしゅう しましょう。

やってみよう
さがして ください

Please look for:
* the words for *what are you doing?*
* the words for *is working, works*
* the word for *photograph*
* the words for *part-time job*
* the words for *is studying, studies*
* the words for *is learning, learns.*

あきのやまに ききましょう

How should I say *My older sister is studying at university?*

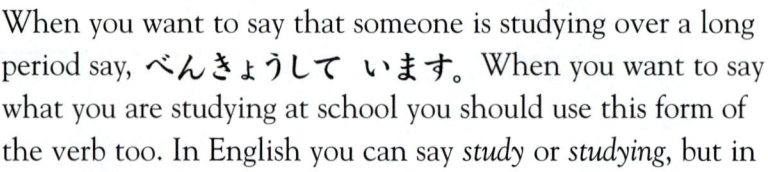

When you want to say that someone is studying over a long period say, べんきょうして います。 When you want to say what you are studying at school you should use this form of the verb too. In English you can say *study* or *studying*, but in Japanese you must say, べんきょうして います (*studying*), not べんきょう します (*study*).

The place where a person studies is followed by particle で. You will learn more about this particle at the bottom of the page. If you want to say, 'My brother is studying at university', this is how you do it: あには だいがくで べんきょうして います.

How do I say *My father works in a bank?*

To say that someone *is working* or *works* say, はたらいて います. Again, it is はたらいて います because the work is performed over a period of time. The place where someone works is also followed by particle で. In this case your sentence will be, 父は ぎんこうで はたらいて います.

What if I want to ask *What are you doing?*

You just say なにを して いますか.

How should I answer this question?

The answer will depend on what you are doing. Do you remember the verb forms you learned with ください? Just replace ください with います. For example: きいて ください (*Please listen*) becomes きいて います (*I am listening*).

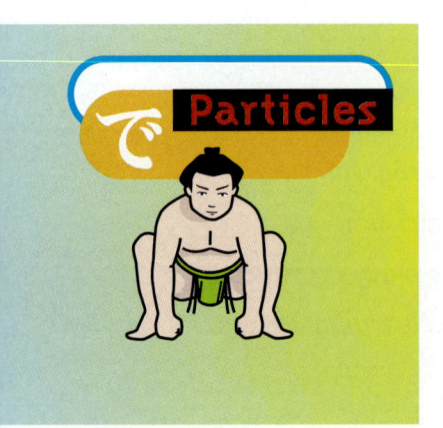

で Particles

Particle で follows the place where someone performs an activity. The verb is always a verb which tells of an activity, not a verb of movement.

18   mirai 2

がんばれ

The underlined words can change.

Asking what someone is doing

<u>なに</u>を して いますか。

Answering

<u>しゃしん</u>を みて います。
<u>ラジオ</u>を きいて います。
_{rajio}
<u>てがみ</u>を かいて います。
<u>まんが</u>を よんで います。
<u>いぬ</u>と あそんで います。
<u>ギター</u>を れんしゅうして います。
_{gitaa}
<u>にほんご</u>を べんきょうして います。

Asking where someone studies

<u>どこ</u>で べんきょうして いますか。

Answering

<u>だいがく</u>で べんきょうして います。
<u>がっこう</u>で べんきょうして います。

Asking where someone works

<u>どこ</u>で はたらいて いますか。

Answering

<u>ぎんこう</u>で はたらいて います。
<u>かいしゃ</u>で はたらいて います。
<u>みせ</u>で はたらいて います。
<u>デパート</u>で はたらいて います。
_{depaato}

Asking what someone studies

<u>なに</u>を べんきょうして いますか。

Answering

<u>にほんご</u>を べんきょうして います。
<u>びじゅつ</u>を べんきょうして います。
<u>れきし</u>を べんきょうして います。
<u>ちり</u>を べんきょうして います。
<u>すうがく</u>を べんきょうして います。
<u>りか</u>を べんきょうして います。
<u>しゃかい</u>を べんきょうして います。

part 1 • unit 2

だれが やりましたか

もう すこし！

1.

2. もしもし。
   はい。まりこです。

3. おとうとさんは なにを して いますか。
   おとうとは、いま、テレビを みて います。

4. お兄さんは なにを して いますか。
   兄は、いま、ラジオを きいて います。

5. おねえさんは なにを して いますか。
   あねは、いま、まんがを よんで います。

6. いとこの こうじくんは なにを して いますか。
   いとこは、いま、べんきょうして います。

7. わたし？ わたしは、いま、うえださんと はなして います。
   まりこさんは なにを して いますか。

やってみよう

1. Make a summary of the activities in which Mariko's family were engaged when Mr Ueda called by completing the sentences below.

   a まりこさんの　おとうとさんは _____。

   b まりこさんの　いとこさんは _____。

   c まりこさんの　お兄さんは _____。

   d まりこさんの　おねえさんは _____。

   e まりこさんは _____。

   Who broke the window? _____ .

2. The members of the basketball team and their coach are scattered around the town today. A TV company wants to locate them all for an interview. Listen to the recorded voice saying where they all are and giving their contact phone numbers. Write the number of the building each of them is in and their phone number next to their name.

   a あきら ( ) ☎ _____   d けん   ( ) ☎ _____

   b つばさ ( ) ☎ _____   e しん   ( ) ☎ _____

   c ひろ   ( ) ☎ _____   f まさお ( ) ☎ _____

part 1 • unit 2

日本からの Eメール

Email　　accessing mailbox...

　こんにちは。おげんきですか。こちらは みんな げんきです。きょうは わたしの かぞくを しょうかい します。わたしの 父(ちち)は かいけいしです。かいしゃで はたらいて います。日(にち)よう日(び)に よく ゴルフ(gorufu)を します。母(はは)は しごとを して いません。でも、ときどき、そふと そぼの みせで はたらきます。

　おとうとの まさひこは ちゅうがく 1ねんせいです。がっこうの クラブ(kurabu)で テニス(tenisu)を して います。わたしは ちゅうがく 3ねんせいです。ことし、わたしは えいごと こくごと しゃかいと りかと すうがくと おんがくと びじゅつと ぎじゅつかていを べんきょうして います。わたしは オーケストラ(ookesutora)で チェロ(chero)を れんしゅうして います。まいにち、れんしゅう します。とても たのしいです。

　じゃ、きょうは これで。てがみを かいて くださいね。

　　　　　　　　　　　　　　　　　　　　　　　　　　さようなら。
　　　　　　　　　　　　　　　　　　　　　　　　　　ゆかり

Can you understand my email? こちら just means *here, on this side*. So we are all well here. My father is an accountant. He works very hard and often comes home quite late. He often (よく) plays golf. My mother does not go to work (しごとを して いません); she stopped work when she had me. My mother's parents have a coffee shop and when it gets busy she sometimes (ときどき) helps out there. She enjoys meeting people, but she says her feet ache. By the way, we use the word みせ for small businesses as well as regular shops.

Notice the way I ended the email too. じゃ、きょうは これで just means *That's all for today*. You can use this in your letters too.

Here are some photos of my grandparent's coffee shop.

22　　mirai 2

I am learning the cello, and I really enjoy practising with the school orchestra. We practise often (よく). Did you notice that when we use まいにち、ときどき and よく the verbs end with ます and not 〜て います。

Here are some examples:

まいにち、がっこうに いきます。	Every day I go to school.
まいにち、いぬと あそびます。	Every day I play with the dog.
ときどき、テレビを みます。	Sometimes I watch TV.
ときどき、ともだちと あそびます。	Sometime I play with my friends.
よく、ピザを たべます。	I often eat pizza.
よく、ともだちと えいがに いきます。	I often go to the movies with friends.

Although we don't go to school every day, we still use まいにち because it *seems* like every day! Until recently we had to go to school on Saturday mornings too. Some schools still open on Saturday mornings.

Our school year starts in April and ends in March. We have a long vacation — six weeks in July and August — and two short vacations. One is at the end of December and the first week of January when we celebrate *Oshōgatsu* (New Year) and the other is at the end of the school year in March/April.

Many schools expect us to continue to go to school during the July/August vacation time to get help from our teachers in our weaker subjects. When you go to Japan you are sure to notice many junior high and senior high school students wearing their uniforms during vacation.

やってみよう

Write a letter to Yukari. Tell her what all the members of your family do. You could also tell her what you do — every day, sometimes and often.

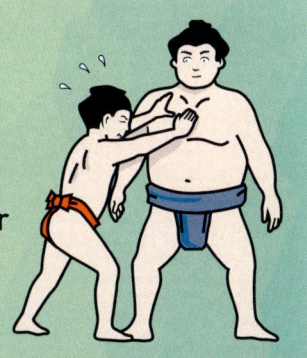

part 1 • unit 2

やってみよう

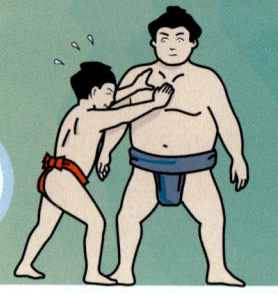

1. Kappa: there are five older people in your family. Using the picture on page 21 decide where they work and complete the table before you start.

Family member	Where they work
お母さん	
お父さん	
お兄さん	
おねえさん	
おじさん	

Answer Tengu's questions with はい or いいえ.

Tengu: find out where the five older members of Kappa's family work in the town illustrated on page 21 by asking questions which Kappa must answer yes or no.

For example:
てんぐ： お母さんは えきで はたらいて いますか。
かっぱ： いいえ、お母さんは えきで はたらいて いません。
てんぐ： お母さんは ぎんこうで はたらいて いますか。
かっぱ： はい。

Complete the table above and compare it with Kappa's. Are they the same?

2. Match the two parts of each snake's body. Choose the beginning part of a sentence from one head then find a suitable ending from a tail.

- しんくんは ギターの せんせいの うちで
- まさしくんは みせで
- ようこさんは だいがくで
- お父さんは かいしゃで
- えりかさんは うちで

- ピアノを れんしゅうして います。
- ギターを ならって います。
- はたらいて います。
- アルバイトを して います。
- えいがの ぎじゅつを べんきょうして います。

3. Complete the following sentences with one of the following particles. (You don't have to use every particle.)

へ　が　で　から　が　を

a　みきさんは にほんの れきし__ べんきょうして います。
b　あした、ケンくんは 日本__ いきます。
c　おばは だいがく__ はたらいて います。
d　ぼくは あね__ 二人 います。
e　おじは きのう、日本__ きました。

mirai 2

クイズ

Check your partner's lifestyle using the following quiz. Tick the statements to which your partner answers yes. Then add up the points using the key at the bottom of the page and find out how well balanced their lifestyle is.

1a よく、おんがくを ききますか。
1b ときどき、おんがくを ききますか。
1c まいにち、おんがくを ききますか。
1d おんがくを ききません。

2a よく、えいがに いきますか。
2b ときどき、えいがに いきますか。
2c まいにち、えいがに いきますか。
2d えいがに いきません。

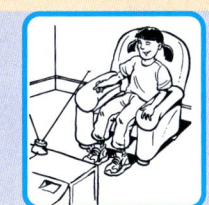

3a よく、テレビを みますか。
3b ときどき、テレビを みますか。
3c まいにち、テレビを みますか。
3d テレビを みません。

4a よく、ともだちと あそびますか。
4b ときどき、ともだちと あそびますか。
4c まいにち、ともだちと あそびますか。
4d ともだちと あそびません。

5a よく、スポーツを しますか。
5b ときどき、スポーツを しますか。
5c まいにち、スポーツを しますか。
5d スポーツを しません。

6a よく、ピザを たべますか。
6b ときどき、ピザを たべますか。
6c まいにち、ピザを たべますか。
6d ピザを たべません。

Key:

1a 3	1b 2	1c 4	1d 1
2a 3	2b 4	2c 1	2d 2
3a 2	3b 4	3c 1	3d 3
4a 4	4b 2	4c 3	4d 1
5a 3	5b 2	5c 4	5d 1
6a 3	6b 4	6c 1	6d 2

How did you rate?

20–24 You have a well-balanced lifestyle.
15–19 You have a fairly well-balanced lifestyle.
6–14 Try doing something different now and then – you'll probably enjoy it!

part 1 • unit 2

やった！

Asking what someone is doing	なに	を	して	います	か。
Saying you are reading (a book)	（ほん	を）	よんで	います。	
you are watching (a movie)	（えいが	を）	みて	います。	
you are listening (to music)	（おんがく	を）	きいて	います。	
you are writing (a letter)	（てがみ	を）	かいて	います。	
you are playing (with the dog)	（いぬ	と）	あそんで	います。	
you are talking (to a friend)	（ともだち	と）	はなして	います。	
you are studying (Japanese)	（にほんご	を）	べんきょうして	います。	
you are learning (guitar)	（ギター	を）	ならって	います。	
you are working			はたらいて	います。	
Asking where someone works	どこ	で	はたらいて	います	か。
Saying someone works at a bank	ぎんこう	で	はたらいて	います。	
Asking where someone is studying	どこ	で	べんきょうして	います	か。
Saying someone is studying at a university	だいがく	で	べんきょうして	います。	
Asking what someone is studying	なに	を	べんきょうして	います	か。
Saying someone is studying music	おんがく	を	べんきょうして	います。	

漢字　かんじ

One way of remembering

母　はは　my mother
　　おかあさん　mother

A seated mother breastfeeds her baby.

兄　あに　my older brother
　　おにいさん　older brother

A mouth on legs — an older brother can often seem like this!

カタカナ

ム mu	ピ pi / ヒ hi / ビ bi	ワ wa	ル ru
ム for movie	ヒ for hinge	ワ for wagging tail	ル for ruins
ニ ni	ア a	パ pa / ハ ha / バ ba	イ i
ニ for knitting needles	ア for avalanche	ハ for hat	イ for insect

ン	ワ	ラ	ヤ	マ	ハ	ナ	タ	サ	カ	ア
	リ		ミ	ヒ	ニ	チ	シ	キ	イ
	ル	ユ	ム	フ	ヌ	ツ	ス	ク	ウ
	レ		メ	ヘ	ネ	テ	セ	ケ	エ
	ロ		ヨ	モ	ホ	ノ	ト	ソ	コ	オ

part 1 • unit 2

カタカナ れんしゅう

1. What do the following people do? Complete the labels by filling in the blank spaces with the appropriate katakana.

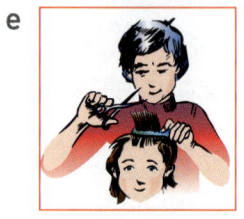

a ☐☐☐ット
      っ

b ス☐☐☐マ☐

c テレ☐ス☐ー
    re

d セー☐ス☐ン
   see

e ヘ☐ドレッサー
   he   resaa

f ☐ーテン☐ー

2. These people only work part-time. Find out what they do by choosing the right katakana words from the list below and writing them in the spaces provided. Then write the English equivalents in the brackets under the spaces.

a _____ で アルバイトを して います。
  (   )

b _____ で アルバイトを して います。
  (   )

c _____ で アルバイトを して います。
  (   )

d _____ で アルバイトを して います。
  (   )

e _____ で アルバイトを して います.
  (   )

f _____ で アルバイトを して います。
  (   )

スーパー   ムービーワールド   タスマニアデパート
ロンドン   パイスタンド   アニーアパート

28   mirai 2

チェック しましょう!

Expressions

きょうは これで	just this for today
こちら	here, this place
それから	after that, and
もちろん	of course

Time words

きょう	today
ことし	this year
ときどき	sometimes
まいにち	every day
よく	often

Places

えき	station
かいしゃ	company
ぎんこう	bank
スーパー suupaa	supermarket
だいがく	university
デパート depaato	department store
としょかん	library
みせ	shop
ムービーワールド muubiiwaarudo	movie world

Verbs

かいて います	am, is, are writing
きいて います	am, is, are listening
しょうかい します	(I) will introduce
ならって います	am, is, are learning
はたらいて います	am, is, are working
はなして います	am, is, are talking
べんきょうして います	am, is, are studying
みて います	am, is, are watching
よんで います	am, is, are reading
れんしゅうして います	am, is, are practising

Nouns

アルバイト arubaito	part-time job (from the German for 'work')
かいけいし	accountant
ぎじゅつ	technology
ゴルフ	golf
ギター	guitar
しごと	work
しゃしん	photo
スター sutaa	celebrity, star
スポーツ	sports
てがみ	letter
チェロ	cello
テレビ	television
ピアノ	piano
バッグスバニー Baggusubanii	Bugs Bunny
ラジオ rajio	radio

I can:
- ask what others are doing now
- say what I am doing now
- ask what others are learning/studying
- say what I am learning/studying
- ask where others do things
- say where I do things
- ask/say where someone works
- read and write a letter about what my family do
- read and write 母 and 兄.

part 1 • unit 2

Unit 3

まさしくんの おばあさんは パラシュートが 好きです
parashuuto 　　　　　す

1
- あした そぼが オーストラリアに きます。
- いいえ、いま、そぼは アメリカに すんでいます。だから、アメリカから きます。
- おばあさんは 日本から きますか。
  にほん

2
- おばあさんは なんさいですか。
- もうすぐ 60さいです。

3
- プレゼントは なにを あげますか。
  purezento
- そぼは しゅげいが 好きです。
  　　　　　　　　　す
- まだ わかりません。カレンさんの おばあさんは なにが 好きですか。
  　　Karen　　　　　　　　　　す

4
- ぼくの そぼは しゅげいは 好き じゃないです。

5
- まさしくんの おばあさんは どんな 人ですか。
- そぼは かっこいい 人です。バイクが だい好きです。
  　　　　　　　　　baiku

30　　mirai 2

6 わたしの 父も バイクが 好きです。そして パラシュートが できます。 (parashuuto)

パラシュート！！ いい かんがえですね。

7 おたんじょうび おめでとう。

うわ！ ありがとう。すばらしい プレゼントですね。 (purezento)

8 おばあさんは だいじょうぶ？

はい、だいじょうぶです。カレンさんも パラシュートが 好きですか。

9 いいえ、きらいです。とても こわいですよ。たなかせんせいは？

ぼくも だいきらいですよ。

10 うわーーい！

おばあさんは パラシュートが 好きですね！

やってみよう
さがして ください

Look for how to say:

* Will soon be 60.
* I don't know yet.
* What present will you give?
* Gran likes handicrafts.
* What kind of person?
* Happy Birthday!
* I hate it!
* That's a good idea!
* It's scary.

part 1 • unit 3   31

あきのやまに ききましょう

Can I use から after any place name to mean *from*?

Yes, you can. Its use and meaning are quite similar to *from* in English, so it's easy to understand. You will learn other things to say with から later.

How should I ask *What do you like*?

You say なにが すきですか. Notice the particle が is used here.

To say what it is that you like, just say the item or thing you like and add が すきです. For example, すしが すきです. If you really like something, say, だいすきです.

Supposing I don't like something?

In this case, you can use the word きらい. Be careful to pronounce it carefully, so that it doesn't sound like きれい (pretty, clean, nice). Again, if you really hate it you can say, だいきらいです. You can also say *I don't like it* by using the negative form. Say すきじゃないです in everyday conversation. じゃ is a contraction of では. In writing and formal speech use, すきでは ありません.

When using the negative, the particle changes to は, as in すしは すきじゃないです. The negative is often used to make contrasting statements. For example, すしが すきです。でも、そばはすきじゃないです. (I like sushi but I don't like soba.)

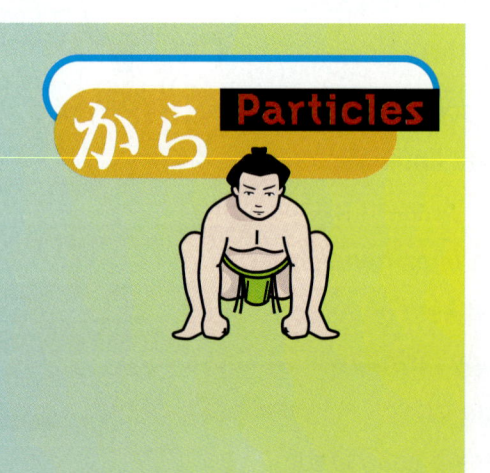

から Particles

The word から, meaning *from*, is another particle. As in English, it can follow either a place or a time.

32 mirai 2

がんばれ

Asking what (food) someone likes

なにが すきですか。

Saying what food you like

てんぷらが すきです。
やきとりが すきです。
すしが すきです。

Asking if someone likes sport

スポーツが すきですか。

Answering yes

はい、(スポーツが) すきです。
はい、(スポーツが) だいすきです。

Answering no

いいえ、(スポーツは) すきじゃないです。
いいえ、(スポーツは) きらいです。
いいえ、(スポーツは) だいきらいです。

Making contrasting statements

れきしが すきです。でも、ちりは きらいです。

Asking if someone can do something

えいごが できますか。

Answering yes

はい、えいごが できます。

Answering no

いいえ、えいごは できません。

Saying someone can do one thing but not another

日本ごが できます。でも、えいごは できません。

Saying which place you come from

シドニーから きました。
Shidonii

オーストラリアから きました。
Oosutoraria

アメリカから きました。
Amerika

part 1 • unit 3

なにが できますか

AB p. 28(1)

もうすこし！

ぼくは やきゅうが できます。	でも、サーフィンは saafin できません。
わたしは しゅげいが できます。	でも、りょうりは できません。
ぼくは 日本ごが できます。 こんにちは。	でも、フランスごは Furansu できません。 Bonjour. Uh!!
わたしは ネットボールが nettoboru できます。	でも、テニスは できません。
ぼくは すいえいが できます。	でも、クリケットは kuriketto できません。

Kappa starts by saying what a well-known person can do.
Tengu completes the statement by saying what they cannot do.
How many statements can you complete in five minutes?

34 mirai 2

どんな人？

Japanese adjectives fall into two groups. Group 1 adjectives all end with い and there is no change before the noun. We will call these い adjectives.

Group 2 adjectives all add な before the noun they describe. We will call these な adjectives. However, there are a few な adjectives, such as きれい and ゆうめい, that also end with い. All な adjectives will appear in the vocabulary lists with な in brackets.

Group 1 examples 〜さんは [い adjective] です。	No change before nouns 〜さんは [い adjective] 人です。
けんくんは かっこいいです。 Ken is cool.	けんくんは かっこいい 人です。 Ken is a cool person.
しんごくんは あたまがいいです。 Shingo is clever.	しんごくんは あたまがいい 人です。 Shingo is a clever person.
エミリーさんは すばらしいです。 Emily is wonderful.	エミリーさんは すばらしい 女の子です。 Emily is a wonderful girl.
たなかせんせいは きびしいです。 Mr Tanaka is strict.	たなかせんせいは きびしい せんせいです。 Mr Tanaka is a strict teacher.

Group 2 examples 〜さんは [な adjective] です。	Add な before nouns 〜さんは [な adjective] な 人です。
つばさくんは げんきです。 Tsubasa is lively.	つばさくんは げんきな おとこの子です。 Tsubasa is a lively boy.
もえさんは きれいです。 Moe is pretty.	もえさんは きれいな 女の子です。 Moe is a pretty girl.
アンさんは しずかです。 Ann is quiet.	アンさんは しずかな 人です。 Ann is a quiet person.
スーさんは しんせつです。 Sue is kind.	スーさんは しんせつな 女の子です。 Sue is a kind girl.

Guess the identity of J.J.

Take turns. Kappa starts. Kappa makes a statement about a classmate using one of the expressions above, using the pseudonym J.J. Tengu guesses who it is by asking a question using the other pattern.

For example:

かっぱ：J.J. くんは あたまがいいです。　　てんぐ：ドンくんは あたまがいい 人ですか。
かっぱ：いいえ、そう じゃないです。　　　てんぐ：ケンくんは あたまがいい 人ですか。
かっぱ：はい、そうです。

part 1　unit 3

どんな ペンパルが いいですか

しんごくんは かっこいい 人です。
ギターが できます。
　gitaa
りょうりが じょうずです。

みきさんは スポーツが 好きな 人です。
　　　　　supootsu　　す
おんがくが 好きです。
りょうりが へたです。

しんくんは あたまがいいです。
べんきょうが 好きです。
スポーツは きらいです。

けんくんは げんきな 人です。
バイクが 好きです。
baiku
すいえいは きらいです。

あきさんは しずかな 人です。
りょうりが できます。
かいものが 好きです。

36　　　　　mirai 2

やってみよう

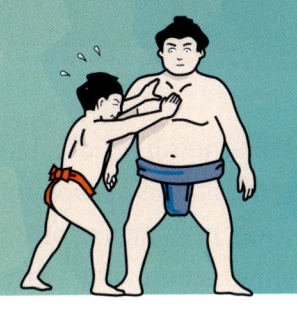

1. Your class is planning a party for your Japanese exchange students. You are asked to find out their food and drink preferences and also what activities they might like to do. Listen to the opinions of Sachiko and Takeshi and fill in the chart.

   ✔✔ loves it   ✔ likes it   ✘ dislikes it   ✘✘ hates it

	さちこ	たけし	じゅん	こうじ	ちえこ
さかな					
ステーキ (suteeki)					
チキン (chikin)					
ハンバーガー (hanbaagaa)					
サラダ (sarada)					
アイスクリーム (aisukuriimu)					
コーラ (koora)					
ミルク (miruku)					
コーヒー (koohii)					
ジュース (juusu)					
テニス (tenisu)					
ダンス (dansu)					
すいえい					
えいが					

2. Write out a popular menu and a schedule of activities that everyone will like.

3. Listen to the exchange students talking and choose a suitable present for each of them.

たけし　じゅん　こうじ　ちえこ　さちこ

part 1 • unit 3

4 You are both members of a band which needs a new member. The person must be able to play a variety of instruments, but should also be able to get along with everyone else.

Kappa, you have interviewed two of the people mentioned below. Use your imagination to circle information about the kind of people they turned out to be. Use a different coloured pen for each person. When you have finished, write down which one you would like to join the band.

Names	Sam, Sue, Jed, Joe, Kim
Personality	lively, clever, quiet, attractive, sports-loving, cool, kind, boring
Home country	America, Canada, Japan, Hong Kong, New Zealand
Can/can't play	trumpet, sax, piano, drums, guitar
Likes/dislikes	Japanese food, Italian food, Indian food, Chinese food, hamburgers
Likes/dislikes	tennis, football, basketball, sport, swimming, golf, shopping

Tengu, you must ask Kappa questions, such as:

サムさんは どんな 人ですか。
Samu

にほんりょうりが 好きですか。

どこから きましたか。

テニスが 好きですか。

ピアノが できますか。
piano

> If Sam has not been selected, Kappa answers わかりません.

Circle the information Kappa gives you. Use a different coloured pen for each person. Did you circle the same things as Kappa? Which of the two do you want to join the band? Is it the same as Kappa's choice?

5 Complete Sachiko's description of her friend Shinichi by choosing suitable words from the box at the bottom of the page.

しんいちくんです。15さいです。げんきな＿＿＿＿＿＿です。すいえいが ＿＿＿＿＿＿。でも、＿＿＿＿＿＿は できません。サッカーが
sakkaa
＿＿＿＿＿＿。好きな かもくは ＿＿＿＿＿＿ ＿＿＿＿＿＿です。
好きな ＿＿＿＿＿＿ は そばです。すしも ＿＿＿＿＿＿。でも、
やきとりは ＿＿＿＿＿＿。わたしは しんいちくんが ＿＿＿＿＿＿。

たべもの	人	できます
サッカー *sakkaa*	だい好きです	しゃかいと びじゅつ
だいきらいです	好きじゃないです	好きです。

38　mirai 2

日本からの Eメール

Email accessing mailbox...

　おはよう！きょうは、おじの かぞくを しょうかい します。かぞくは 4人です。おじと おばと いとこの あきらと みわです。あきらは おとこの子です。みわは 女の子です。

　4人は いま、オーストラリアに すんで います。おじは 日本の かいしゃで はたらいて います。おばは こうこうで 日本ごを おしえて います。みんな オーストラリアが だい好きです。オーストラリアの たべものも だい好きです。

　あきらは ちゅうがく 3ねんせいです。みわは ちゅうがく 1ねんせいです。あきらは 日本ごが できます。でも、みわは 日本ごは あまり できません。みわは がっこうで ドイツごを べんきょうして います。

　おばは しゅげいが 好きです。でも、みわと あきらは しゅげいは 好きでは ありません。スポーツが 好きです。おじも スポーツが だい好きです。じゃ、きょうは これで。てがみを かいて くださいね。

　　　　　　　　　　　　　　　　　　　　　　　さようなら。ゆかり

Hi! Can you understand my letter? I have two uncles and aunts and four cousins. The ones I told you about today live in Australia. My cousin Miwa was born in Australia and she can't speak much Japanese. She can understand a bit. When she visited us last year, everyone chatted away to her in Japanese but she didn't understand everything. By the way, あまり できません means *can't do much*. Use it when you want to say you are not very good at something. For example, if you're not very good at swimming, you can say すいえいは あまり できません. Notice that we use the particle は in this case. The following photos are of some of the things that I like to do.

わたしは スキーが 好きです。いま、れんしゅうして います。

わたしは うみが 好きです。
母も うみが 好きです。
でも、すいえいは あまり できません。

やってみよう

Write a letter to Yukari. Tell her what you like and dislike and what members of your family can and can't do very well.

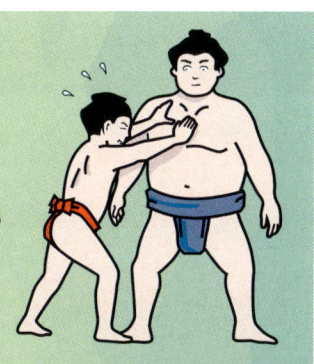

part 1 • unit 3

← えみこ

いとこの えみこと えみこの ともだちの まりこです。2人は ちゅうがく 3ねんせいです。えみこは やさしい 人です。よく、こうえんで こどもと あそびます。おんがくと びじゅつが よく できます。まりこは あたまが いいです。がっこうが だい好きです。まりこは まいにち べんきょう します。りかと すうがくが よく できます。

じゅん →

わたしの いとこの じゅんと じゅんの ともだちです。3人は こうこう 2ねんせいです。じゅんは かっこいい 人です。ギターが じょうずです。サーフィンと スキーが できます。じゅんは じょうだんが 好きです。ともだちは みんな じゅんが 好きです。

やった！

Asking what someone likes Saying you like something	なに [Thing]	が が	好き （だい）好き	です です。	か。
Saying that you don't like something	[Thing]	は	好き じゃ 好き では 好き では	ないです。 ないです。 ありません。	
Saying that you dislike something	[Thing]	は	（だい）きらい	です。	
Asking if someone can do something Saying that you can do something Saying that you can't do something	[Thing] [Thing] [Thing]	が が は	できます できます。 できません。	か。	
Saying where someone came from	[Place]	から	きました。		

漢字　かんじ

One way of remembering

女　おんな　woman — The figure of a kneeling woman.

子　こども　child — Many babies are carried in a special support like a pouch on their mother's back in Japan.

好　すき like, love / すきな favourite — The emotions of like and love are portrayed as a woman and child together.

part 1 • unit 3

カタカナ

ラ ra	シ shi / ジ ji	ユ yu	フ fu / プ pu / ブ bu
ラ for raft	シ for shiver	ユ for utility truck	フ for footstool
レ re	セ se / ゼ ze	ク ku / グ gu	リ ri
レ for reindeer	セ for cemetery	ク for cook	リ for river

ン ワ ラ ヤ マ ハ ナ タ サ カ ア
　リ　ミ ヒ ニ チ シ キ イ
ル ユ ム フ ヌ ツ ス ク ウ
レ　　メ ヘ ネ テ セ ケ エ
ロ ヨ モ ホ ノ ト ソ コ オ

カタカナ れんしゅう

1 Circle all the sport-related words in katakana and join each of them with the appropriate picture.

トニー　　クーラー　　テニス　　テーブル　　ロデオ
パン　　ランニング　アルバイト　パラシュート　ビール

2 Complete the appropriate country's name in katakana under each of the flags by filling in the blanks.

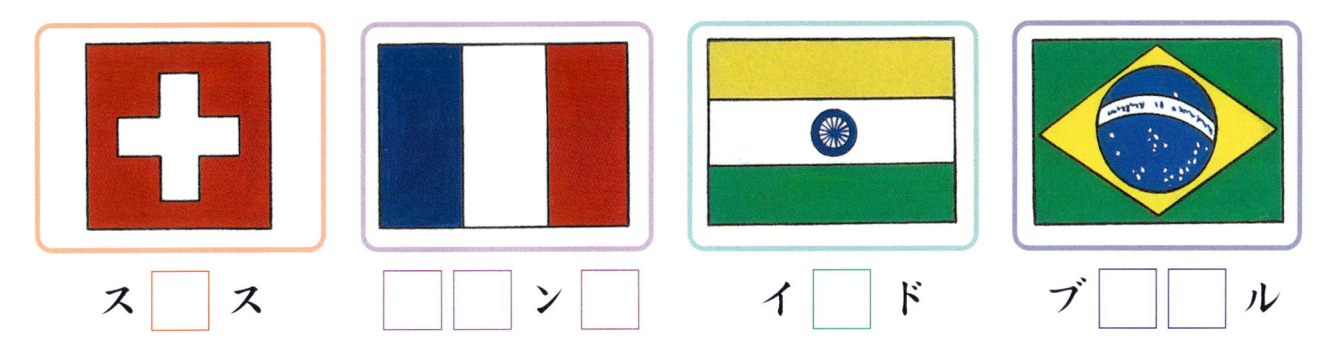

ス☐ス　　☐☐ン☐　　イ☐ド　　ブ☐☐ル

3 Look at this huge gift-wrapped box! All you have to do to receive this present is to complete the names of all the items inside and on the label attached to it in katakana.

part 1 • unit 3

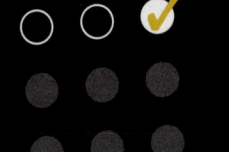

チェック しましょう！

AB pp. 32, 33

Like and dislike

きらいです	hate, dislike
好きです	like
好きじゃないです	don't like
好きでは ありません	don't like (formal style)
だいきらいです	dislike very much
だい好きです	like very much

Expressions

あまり できません	can't do much
いい かんがえ	good idea
まだ わかりません	don't know yet
もうすぐ	soon
よく できます	does well

Congratulations

おたんじょうび おめでとう(ございます)	Happy birthday!

Question words

どんな	what kind of

Exclamation

うわあい！	Wow!

Nouns

おとこの子(こ)	boy
女の子(おんなのこ)	girl
かいもの	shopping
かんがえ	idea
しゅげい	handicraft
バイク	motorbike
パラシュート	parachute
プレゼント	present
りょうり	dishes, cooking
サッカー sakkaa	soccer

Verbs

あげます	give
できます	can do
できません	can't do
わかりません	don't know

Adjectives

いい	good
あたまがいい	clever
こわい	scary
すばらしい	wonderful
じょうず(な)	skilled, good at
しずか(な)	quiet
とても	very
へた(な)	unskilled, poor at

I can:
- ask what others like and dislike
- say what I like and dislike
- say what I like a lot
- say what I dislike a lot
- say what I can do
- say what I can't do
- describe my friends and family
- say Happy birthday!
- read and write what I can say, as well as 子, 女 and 好き.

part 2

Animals are friends too

At the end of Part 2 you will be able to:

- say where things are
- describe the different parts of a house
- describe pets
- describe other animals
- count animals.

You will also find out about some unusual Japanese pets and learn some more katakana and kanji.

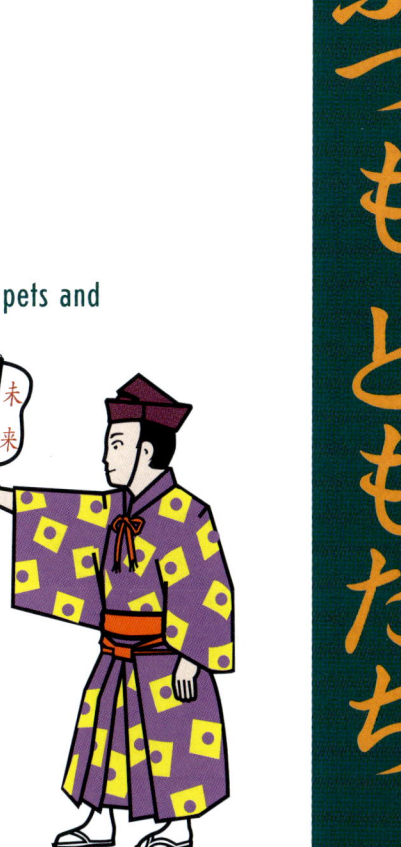

どうぶつも ともだち

Unit 4

まさしくんの うちは おもしろい

1. あっ。あれは ぼくの こいのぼりです！ぼくの うちに いきましょうか。
   ええ、いきましょう。

2. 大きい こいのぼりですね。
   きれいな こいのぼりですね。

3. こんにちは。
   ただいま！
   おかえりなさい。あら、こんにちは。

4. げんかんで くつを ぬいで ください。そして、スリッパを はいて ください。
   surippa
   へんな スリッパですね。あまり 大きくないですね。

5. まさしくんの へやに なにが ありますか。
   まさしくんの へやに なにが いますか。
   チュ... チュ...
   Enter at your own risk!
   SQUEAK SQUEAK

6. ねずみが います。ぼくの ペットです。
   petto
   ねずみ？ へんな ペットですね。
   へんじゃないです。

46　mirai 2

やってみよう

さがして ください

* the word for a carp-shaped kite
* the word for shoes
* the words for *strange slippers*
* the words for big and small
* the word for a mouse
* the word for cute or sweet
* how to say *It's not cute*
* how to ask *What is in your room?*

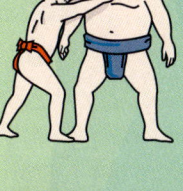

part 2 • unit 4

あきのやまに ききましょう

What is the difference between あります and います?

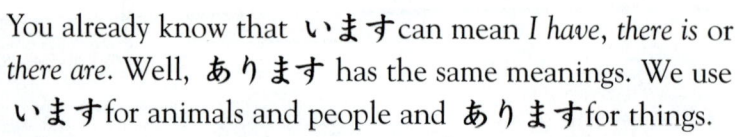

You already know that います can mean *I have*, *there is* or *there are*. Well, あります has the same meanings. We use います for animals and people and あります for things. For example, へやに ねずみが います (*There is* a mouse in the room), へやに つくえが あります (*There is* a desk in the room).

What is the difference between これ, それ and あれ?

They are similar in meaning to *this*, *that* and *that over there*. これ indicates something near the speaker; それ indicates something near the listener; and あれ, something at a distance from both.

In English you often say *it* instead of *that*. For example, in answer to the question, 'What is this?' (the item being near the speaker), you often answer, 'It is a present'.

In Japanese, we *always* use これ and それ. For example, the answer to the question, これは なんですか, would be それは プレゼントです.

It is the same with the question, 'What is that?' (the item being at a distance from both speakers). In English you might answer, 'It is a mouse'. In Japanese we would use あれ for both the question and the answer: あれは なんですか; あれは ねずみです.

What are *koinobori*?

They are colourful carp-shaped kites, attached to bamboo poles, which we fly in Japan to celebrate Children's Day on May 5. It used to be a boys' festival and the carp was chosen as a symbol for a boy's strong, good health because carp can swim against the current and live a long time.

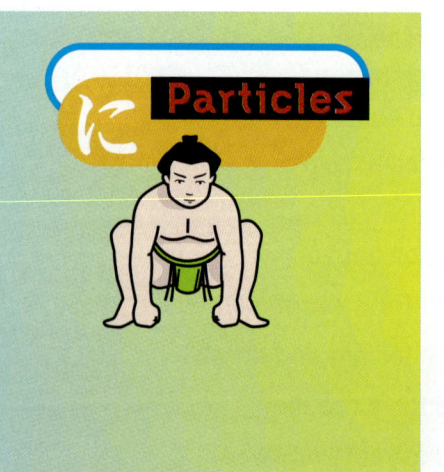

に Particles

Particle に can mean *in* or *on* when it follows a place. The verb used can be either います or あります.

Place に thing が あります。 います。

Thing は place に あります。 います。

48 mirai 2

がんばれ

Asking what is in a place

Animate object

What is in the <u>room</u>?
<u>へや</u>に なにが いますか。

Inanimate object

What is in the <u>garden</u>?
<u>にわ</u>に なにが ありますか。

Saying what is in a place

There is a <u>mouse</u> in the room.
へやに <u>ねずみ</u>が います。

There is (are) a <u>chair</u> (<u>chairs</u>) in the <u>garden</u>.
<u>にわ</u>に <u>いす</u>が あります。

Asking where someone or an animal is

Where is your <u>older brother</u>?
<u>お兄さん</u>は どこに いますか。

Where is the <u>dog</u>?
<u>いぬ</u>は どこに いますか。

Saying where someone or an animal is

He (older brother) is in the <u>house</u>.
兄は <u>うち</u>に います。

It (the dog) is in the garden.
いぬは <u>にわ</u>に います。

Asking where something is

Where is the <u>phone</u>?
<u>でんわ</u>は どこに ありますか。

Saying where something is

It (the phone) is in the <u>living room</u>.
でんわは <u>いま</u>に あります。

Asking about things near to the speaker

What is this?
これは なんですか。

Answering

It is <u>sushi</u>.
それは <u>すし</u>です。

Asking about things near to the listener

What is that?
それは なんですか。

Answering

It is <u>soba</u> (noodles).
これは <u>そば</u>です。

Asking about things distant from both speakers

What is that (over there)?
あれは なんですか。

Answering

It is a <u>carp-shaped kite</u>.
あれは <u>こいのぼり</u>です。

Indicating things near to the speaker

This is a present.
これは プレゼントです。

Indicating things at a distance from both

That is big, isn't it?
あれは おおきい ですね。

Indicating things near to the listener

Please show me that.
それを みせて ください。

part 2 • unit 4

ぼくの うちは 大きくないです

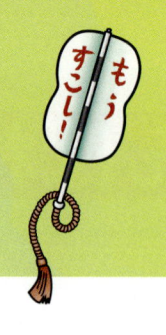

In Unit 3 you learned how to use い and な adjectives. Here you will find out how to use adjectives in the negative form.

1　い adjectives　　Simply drop off the final い and add くないです, like this:
　　　　　　　　　　　ぼくの うちは 小さ~~い~~です ＋ くないです.

Affirmative	Negative
ぼくの へびは かわいいです。 My snake is cute.	おとうとの へびは かわいくないです。 My brother's snake isn't cute.
ドンくんの ねこは きたないです。 Don's cat is dirty.	わたしの ねこは きたなくないです。 My cat isn't dirty.
日本ごは むずかしいです。 Japanese is difficult.	日本ごは むずかしくないです。 Japanese isn't difficult.

2　な adjectives　　Simply add じゃないです, like this:
　　　　　　　　　　　ぼくの うちは きれい~~です~~ ＋ じゃないです.

Affirmative	Negative
ひろくんの スリッパは へんです。 Hiro's slippers are strange.	ぼくの スリッパは へんじゃないです。 My slippers aren't strange.
くみこさんは きれいです。 Kumiko is pretty.	くみこさんは きれいじゃないです。 Kumiko isn't pretty.
いまは しずかです。 The living room is quiet.	いまは しずかじゃないです。 The living room isn't quiet.

3　い adjectives or な adjectives ＋ noun です

Simply add じゃないです to the noun, like this:
　　ねこは 大きい どうぶつ~~です~~ ＋ じゃないです.
　　すずきさんは ゆうめいな 人~~です~~ ＋ じゃないです.

Affirmative	Negative
やまださんは いい 人です。 Mr Yamada is a good person.	やまださんは いい 人 じゃないです。 Mr Yamada isn't a good person.
へびは かわいい どうぶつです。 The snake is a cute animal.	へびは かわいい どうぶつ じゃないです。 The snake isn't a cute animal.
まゆみさんは へんな 人です。 Mayumi is a strange person.	まゆみさんは へんな 人 じゃないです。 Mayumi isn't a strange person.
コアラは げんきな どうぶつです。 The koala is a lively animal.	コアラは げんきな どうぶつ じゃないです。 The koala isn't a lively animal.

やってみよう

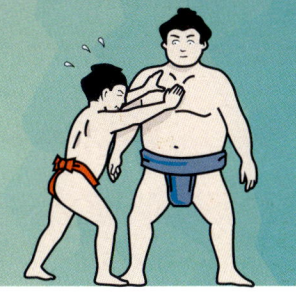

あまのじゃく ゲーム

Amanojaku is the name of a cheeky Japanese elf who annoys people by insisting on saying the opposite of what they say.

For example, if someone says, 'This is nice', Amanojaku will say, 'This is not nice'.

Tengu makes sentences using the Amida kuji method to find the end of the sentence. (see *Mirai Stage 1*, page 25). Kappa pretends to be Amanojaku and says the opposite (the negative) of what Tengu has said. If Kappa says it correctly Tengu starts to draw the face of Amanojaku in a notebook following the steps shown below, like when you play 'Hangman'.

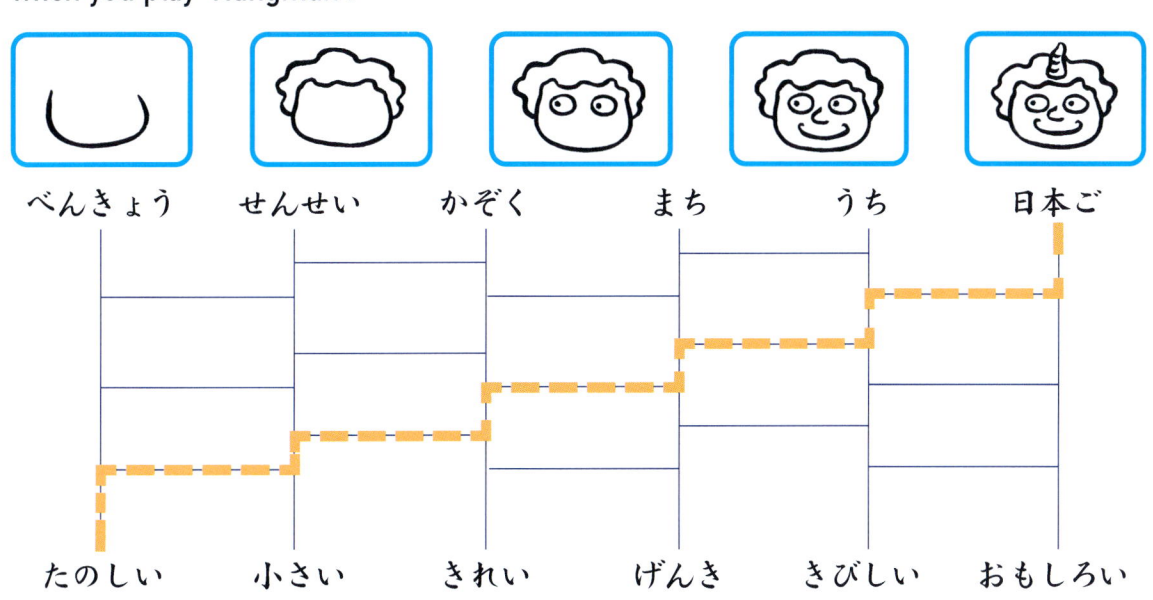

べんきょう	せんせい	かぞく	まち	うち	日本ご
たのしい	小さい	きれい	げんき	きびしい	おもしろい

For example:

日本ごは たのしいです。 ➡ 日本ごは たのしくないです。

Now it's Tengu's turn to pretend to be Amanojaku.

かいもの	ねこ	ひろくん	こうえん	りょうり
しずか	むずかしい	かわいい	しんせつ	おもしろい

part 2 • unit 4

しんいちくんの うち

- ベランダ (beranda)
- わしつ
- しんいちくんの へや
- おねえさんの へや
- とり
- しょうじ
- ねこ
- ほんだな
- ふとん
- ベッド (beddo)
- たたみ
- だいどころ
- (お)ふろば
- おてあらい (トイレ)
- いま
- げんかん
- シャワー (shawaa)
- テレビ
- くつばこ
- テーブル
- (お)ふろ
- ソファー (sofaa)
- スリッパ
- かめ
- へび
- さかな
- かだん
- いけ
- にわ
- き
- うさぎ
- もん

やってみよう

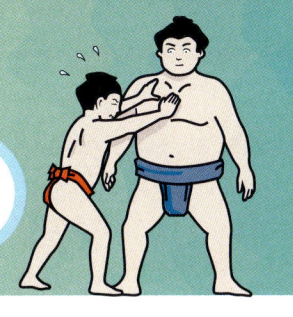

パズル

1. Dean sent an email to his friend Shinichi. He asked lots of questions about Shinichi's house and garden. Below you will find Shinichi's answers, but what were the questions?
   a にわに かめと うさぎと いぬが います。
   b いまに ソファーと テレビが あります。
   c あねの へやに ベッドと つくえと いすが あります。
   d たたみと しょうじは わしつに あります。
   e ねこは ぼくの へやに います。

2. Look at the picture of Shinichi's house and see if you can answer the following questions.
   a お父さんは どこに いますか。
   b スリッパは どこに ありますか。
   c だいどころに なにが ありますか。
   d (お)ふろは どこに ありますか。
   e お母さんは どこに いますか。

3. Katie was asked by her host family to look after the pets, but where are they? Listen and put a tick if the clue is correct and a cross if it is incorrect.
   a The dog is in the garden. _____
   b The tortoise is in the bathroom. _____
   c The cat is in the older sister's room. _____
   d The mouse is in the kitchen. _____
   e The rabbit is in the toilet. _____
   f The bird is in the living room. _____

4. Sue, Shingo and Emily have just finished drawing plans of their rooms, but they have forgotten to write their names on the plans. Listen to each of them describing their rooms. Can you work out which plan belongs to which student? Label three of the plans with the correct owners' names.

part 2 • unit 4

ホームステイの うちで
At the home-stay house

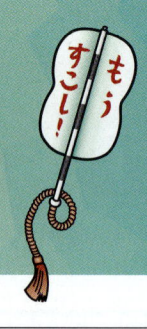

いまで
- これは なんですか。
- それは とうふです。

にわで
- あれは なんですか。
- あれは こいのぼりです。

げんかんで
- ぼくの スリッパは どれですか。
- これですよ。

Complete the following dialogues with これ、それ、あれ or どれ.

a
- ___ を みせて ください。
- ___ ?
- いいえ、___ です。

b
- ___ を みせて ください。
- えっ？ ___ ですか。
- はい、___ です。
- ___ ですか。

やってみよう

1 What did Kengo say?

Your friend has only just started to learn Japanese, but is soon going to Japan with a music group. She sent you this note with a cassette tape. Listen to what Kengo said and write a reply.

> Hi! I have received a recorded letter from Kengo. Kengo is my host brother. His family is going to host me when I go there in December. I don't quite understand what he says. Can you help me?
>
> These are the things I want to know.
> - What kind of place do they live in?
> - How many people are in the family and what they are like?
> - Do they have any pets? I am a bit worried because I am allergic to cats.
> - I am thinking of giving Kengo a book about Australia. Do you think that would be a good idea?
> - Do they understand English? Should I study hard before going?

2 ペット　コンテスト

Tengu: You are the compere of a pet contest and you will be introducing the owners and pets to the judges. First you have to ask Kappa which pet belongs to each entrant in the table below. There are two of each kind of pet, so you will have to ask Kappa to describe each pet. When you have identified the pet, put the identifying letter from the illustration next to the owner's name in the table.

Kappa: You are the organiser of a pet contest and you know who owns each of the pets in the illustration. Decide which of the pets is owned by each of the entrants in the table Write the pet's identifying letter next to the owner's name. Tengu will ask you which pet each entrant owns. First say what kind of pet it is and then what it is doing. When you have finished, compare tables. Are they the same?

Once you have found which pet belongs to whom, you can introduce all the pets to the judges and audience. Take turns.

This is how you might get started.

てんぐ: まさしくんの ペットは なんですか。
かっぱ: かめです。
てんぐ: どれですか。
かっぱ: あれです。ねています。
てんぐ: あれは g ですね。3ばんです。

Entrant	Identifying letter
Monica	
Ken	
Masashi	
Nikki	
Hiro	

55

日本からの Eメール

Email — accessing mailbox...

こんにちは。おげんきですか。わたしの うちは きょうとに あります。えきから あるいて 15ふんです。とても しずかな ところです。わたしの うちは ふるいです。でも、大きいです。小さい にわも あります。わたしの へやと おとうとの まさひこの へやは 大きくないです。わたしの へやに ベッドと つくえと いすと たんすと ほんだなが あります。わたしは まいにち、そうじを します。だから、いつも きれいです。まさひこは そうじを しません。だから、まさひこの へやは とても きたないです。

うちに いぬが います。なまえは チャポです。チャポは いつも わたしの へやで ねます。まさひこの へやで ねません。チャポは きれいな へやが 大好きです。

ゆかり

Did you understanding everything? Did you guess that そうじします means to clean or tidy? Masahiko has a very きたない room but he likes it like that.

Our house, being old, has several Japanese-style rooms. We call these rooms わしつ and they have very little furniture in them. Japanese-style rooms have *tatami* on the floor and the windows are covered with sliding screens called *shōji*. There is a *tokonoma*, or alcove, for displaying a beautiful scroll. My mother changes the scroll according to the season. The *shōji* are made of a light wooden frame, with slats of wood forming rectangular 'window panes'. These 'window panes' are covered with thin white paper which is translucent, so light can come into the room but no one can see in, so we don't need curtains.

とこのま

Tatami mats measure about 90 centimetres by 180 centimetres each. They are made of compressed straw about five centimetres thick and have a smooth woven covering made from rush. A decorative fabric tape runs down the long side of each mat. The mats are very comfortable to sit, walk and sleep on. In fact, each mat is just big enough for one person to sleep on. We measure the sizes of rooms according to the number of mats that can be fitted in to them.

In a *tatami* room, we sit on large cushions called *zabuton*, and sleep on the *tatami* on a futon which we spread out on the floor at night.

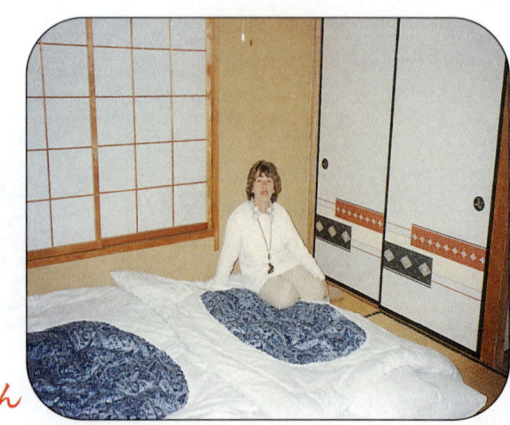

しょうじ と ふとん

mirai 2

Tatami rooms are very useful, because they can be used for lots of purposes. The futons are folded up and placed in a deep cupboard during the day. Then the room can be used for entertaining visitors, for playing games or watching TV. In some *tatami* rooms there is a special shrine called a *butsudan* in remembrance of relatives who have died. We keep photographs of them in the shrine and often say a little prayer for them.

Everyone in Japan takes their shoes off at the *genkan*. We think it is very dirty to bring the dirt from the street into the house. All Japanese *genkan* have a slipper rack and a box to place outdoor shoes in. If the house is entirely Western style, everyone wears slippers everywhere in the house. When someone visits the toilet they leave these slippers outside the door and use special toilet slippers which are kept inside the toilet.

If the house has *tatami* rooms, everyone removes their slippers before walking on the *tatami*. This is because we think of the *tatami* as you think of your bed, and we want it to be kept very clean. Also, the soles of slippers may roughen the smooth woven surface.

ぶつだん

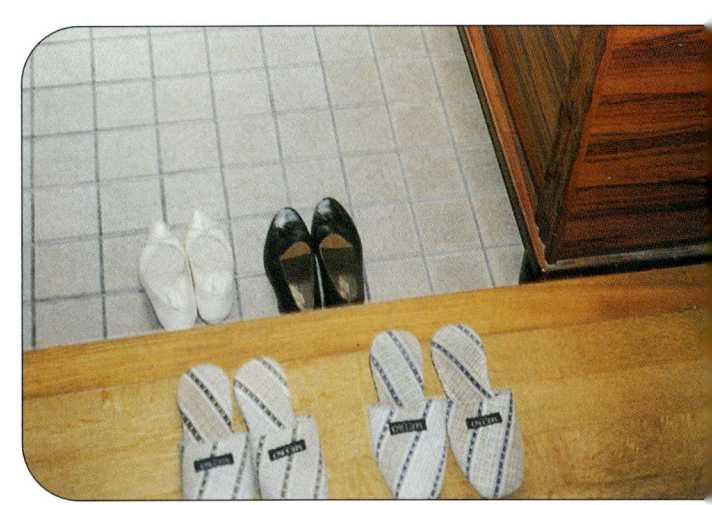

げんかん

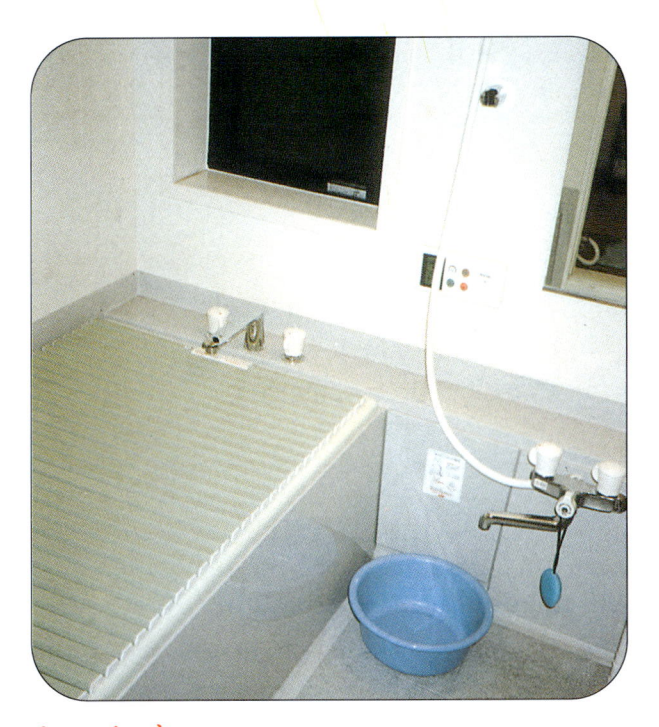

Japan is blessed with lots of hot springs, so it has long been our tradition to enjoy soaking in hot water. No matter how small the apartment, we have a very deep bath that we can relax in. Every evening the bath is filled with hot water and a cover is placed on top to keep the heat in. We take our clothes off in a small room attached to the bathroom before entering the steamy bathroom. The bathroom floor is lower than the rest of the house and the whole room is waterproof so we can splash water around as much as we like. We wash ourselves outside the bath and then get into the bath to relax in the steaming water. We never use soap or washers inside the bath. The hot water is only for relaxing in and nobody wants to make it dirty for the next bather.

おふろば

やった！

Asking what is in a place (animate object)	[Place]	に	なに	が	います	か。
Saying what is in a place (animate object)	[Place]	に	[animate object]	が	います。	
Asking what is in a place (inanimate object)	[Place]	に	なに	が	あります	か。
Saying what is in a place (inanimate object)	[Place]	に	[inanimate object]	が	あります。	
Asking where someone/an animal is	[Person/animal]	は	どこ	に	います	か。
Saying where someone/an animal is	[Person/animal]	は	[place]	に	います。	
Asking where something is	[Thing]	は	どこ	に	あります	か。
Saying where something is	[Thing]	は	[place]	に	あります。	
Asking about things near to the speaker	これは	なん	です	か。		
Answering (the listener answers)	それは	[thing]	です。			
Asking about things near to the listener	それは	なん	です	か。		
Answering (the listener answers)	これは	[thing]	です。			
Asking about things at a distance	あれは	なん	です	か。		
Answering (the listener answers)	あれは	[thing]	です。			
Indicating something near to the speaker	これ					
Indicating something near to the listener	それ	[particle]	[rest of sentence].			
Indicating something at a distance to both	あれ					

漢字　かんじ

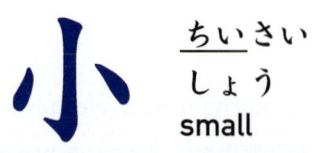

One way of remembering

大 — おおきい / だい — big, large

This 人 is telling about a fish he once caught. It was as big as his outstretched arms.

小 — ちいさい / しょう — small

When his friends start to make fun of him, he shyly moves his hands in and says, 'Well, actually, it was this small.'

カタカナ

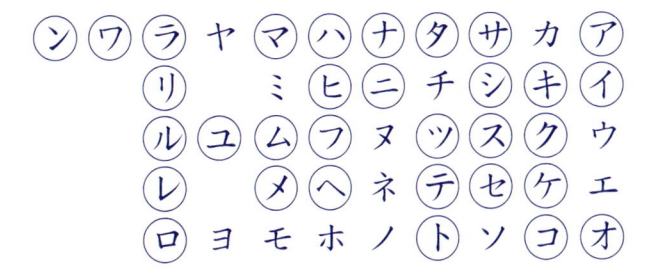

ツ tsu	ペ pe / ヘ he / ベ be	ケ ke / ゲ ge	サ sa / ザ za
ツ for toothpick	ヘ for headache	ケ for kettle	サ for sapphire
ナ na	メ me	キ ki / ギ gi	コ ko / ゴ go
ナ for nutcracker	メ for melon	キ for kimono	コ for cocoa

ア イ ウ エ オ
カ キ ク ケ コ
サ シ ス セ ソ
タ チ ツ テ ト
ナ ニ ヌ ネ ノ
ハ ヒ フ ヘ ホ
マ ミ ム メ モ
ヤ　ユ　ヨ
ラ リ ル レ ロ
ワ
ン

part 2 • unit 4

カタカナ れんしゅう

1 Look at these advertisements from a pet shop and answer the following questions.

ドリップシート猫用 198円	ヘルシージャーキー 798円	アンダーシート 498円	チャム 698円
ペット用サマーベッド 1,580円	デオシート 1,780円	ドッグフード 798円 ゴールド	ブレッキーズ 598円

a How much are 'Brekkies'?
b How much is 'Healthy Jerky'?
c Which dog food is more expensive, 'Gold' or 'Chum'?
d Which is most expensive, 'Drip Sheet', 'Under Sheet' or 'Deo Sheet'?
e For ¥1580 what can you buy for your pet?

2 You're going to buy a puppy. Circle what you need to get beforehand in the list below.

a ラビットフード   b ピザ   c アイスクリーム
d スリッパ   e ドッグフード   f ペットベッド

3 Connect the katakana words with their English equivalents.

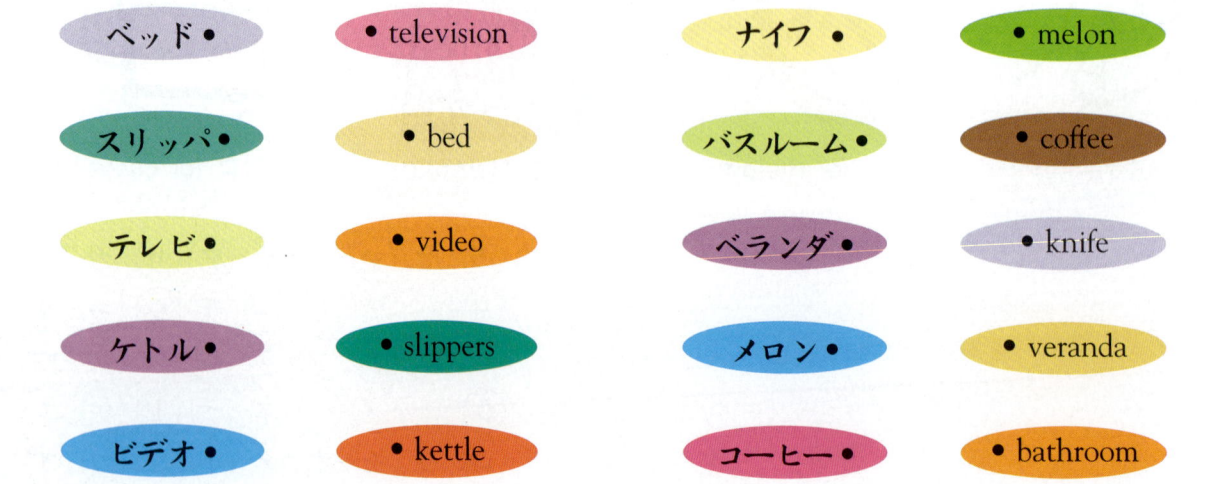

ベッド •   • television   ナイフ •   • melon
スリッパ •   • bed   バスルーム •   • coffee
テレビ •   • video   ベランダ •   • knife
ケトル •   • slippers   メロン •   • veranda
ビデオ •   • kettle   コーヒー •   • bathroom

60   mirai 2

チェック しましょう！

Adjectives

大きい（おおきい）	big, large
かわいい	cute, lovely, sweet
かわいそう（な）	sad, poor, pitiable
きたない	dirty, messy
小さい（ちいさい）	small
へん（な）	strange, odd, unusual
ふるい	old

Verbs

あります	there is/are/exists (inanimate)
います	there is/are/exists (animate)
そうじします	make clean
ぬぎます	take off, remove
ぬいで ください	please remove
はきます	wear (shoes, jeans, skirt)
はいて ください	please wear
だします	take, put, put out
だしても いいですか	May I take it out?

Things inside and outside the house

いけ	pond	ソファー	sofa
かだん	flower bed	たたみ	woven, rush mats
木（き）	tree	たんす	chest of drawers
くつ	shoe(s)	テーブル	table
くつばこ	shoe cupboard	にわ	garden
こいのぼり	carp-shaped kite	ベッド	bed
しょうじ	sliding screen	ふとん	futon
スリッパ	slippers	ほんだな	bookcase

In the house

いま	living room
おてあらい（トイレ）	toilet
（お）ふろば, （お）ふろ	bathroom, bath
げんかん	entrance hall
シャワー	shower
だいどころ	kitchen
へや	room
ベランダ	veranda
もん	gate
わしつ	Japanese-style room

Animals

うさぎ	rabbit	ねこ	cat
かめ	tortoise	ねずみ	mouse, rat
とり	bird	ペット	pet
どうぶつ	animal	へび	snake

Identifying words

あれ	that (one) over there
これ	this (one)
それ	that (one)
どれ	Which one?

Noun

ところ	place

I can:
- say where things are
- say where animals and people are
- describe some pets
- identify which one
- describe my house
- read and write a description of a house
- read and write 大きい and 小さい.

part 2 • unit 4

Unit 5

へびも かえるが 好き

1．
- かわいい!! なんびき いますか。
- 20ぴきぐらい います。ぼくは かえるが 大好きです。

2．
- あの かえるは 目が あかいですね。
- この かえるは 目が きいろいですね。

3．
- あしが ながいですね。
- ても ながいですね。
- ほんとう!

4．
- かえるは なにを たべますか。

5．
- かや はえ など、いろいろな むしを たべます。

62　mirai 2

6 あれは とても 大きい かえる ですね。

あれは ひきがえるです。むかしは みなみアメリカに いました。いまは オーストラリアにも います。

7 かわいくないですね。みにくいですね。

いやですね。

そうですね。それに、この ひきがえるの からだには どくが あります。

8 あら！こわい！へびです。

その へびは だいじょうぶです。どくへびじゃないです。こわくないです。

9 うわ！ かわいそう！

でも、へびも かえるが 大好きですね。

10 そして、わらいかわせみは へびが 大好きです。

やってみよう

さがして ください

* the word for frog
* the word for cane toad
* the counter for animals
* how to say *It has red eyes*
* how to say *Its body is poisonous*
* how to say *It has long legs*
* the words for *poisonous snake*
* how to say *It eats mosquitoes, flies and so on*
* the word for kookaburra
* how to say *Snakes like frogs a lot too.*

part 2 • unit 5   63

あきのやまに ききましょう

Why do you say なんびき when asking how many animals there are?

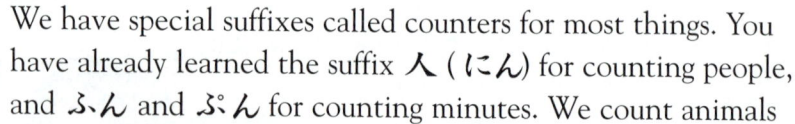

We have special suffixes called counters for most things. You have already learned the suffix 人 (にん) for counting people, and ふん and ぷん for counting minutes. We count animals using the suffix ひき. There are phonetic changes to watch out for, but you really only need to know a few to be able to say how many pets you have. You'll find a list on page 66.

What is the difference between この, その and あの, and これ, それ and あれ?

The words この, その and あの come before the thing you are talking about to indicate its position relative to the speaker and listener. The words mean *this ~*, *that ~*, and *that ~ over there*. The words これ, それ and あれ are used on their own.

What is the difference between あの かえるは めが あかいです and あの かえるの めは あかいです?

The first sentence means *That frog has red eyes*; the second sentence means *That frog's eyes are red*. You can use either sentence pattern depending on what you want to say.

What do にも and には mean?

These are double particles. In each case, the particles have the same meaning as they would have by themselves. So オーストラリアにも means *also in Australia*. The particle に corresponds to *in*, and the particle も corresponds to *also*.

In the case of には, as in the phrase からだには, the two particles again keep their normal meanings: に means *on* and は indicates the topic. So the phrase means *As for on the body*.

Double particles are very common; just think of the basic meaning of each of them and it will be easy to understand the meaning.

や Particles

You already know that the particle と between nouns means *and*. Particle や means *and other things*. We often make it even clearer by adding など, which means *and so on*.

Just the things mentioned

These things and others

miraí 2

がんばれ

Commenting on particular things near the speaker

この かえるは 大きいです。
This frog is big.

Commenting on particular things near the listener

その へびは こわいです。
That snake is scary.

Commenting on particular things at a distance from both speakers

あの ひきがえるは みにくいです。
That cane toad is ugly.

Asking how many animals there are/someone has

いぬは なんびき いますか。
How many dogs are there?
How many dogs do you have?

Answering

いぬは 2ひき います。
There are two.
I have two.

Describing parts of a whole

その いぬは めが 大きいです。   or   その いぬの めは 大きいです。
That dog has big eyes.   That dog's eyes are big.

ケンくんは かみが くろいです。   or   ケンくんの かみは くろいです。
Ken has black hair.   Ken's hair is black.

Asking someone to say the colour of something.

なにいろの とりですか。
What colour bird is it?

Saying the colour of something

あかい とりです。   It is a red bird.
きいろい(きいろの) とりです。   It is a yellow bird.
みどりの(みどりいろの) とりです。   It is a green bird.

part 2 • unit 5

なんびき いますか

一ぴき いっぴき		二ひき にひき	
三びき さんびき		四ひき よんひき	
五ひき ごひき		六ぴき ろっぴき	
七ひき ななひき		八ぴき はっぴき	
九ひき きゅうひき		十ぴき じゅっぴき	

Note: **P** indicates ぴき, **B** indicates びき and **H** indicates ひき sound.

パズル 1

a　うさぎは なんびき いますか。
b　かえるは なんびき いますか。
c　ひつじは なんびき いますか。
d　やぎは なんびき いますか。
e　かめは なんびき いますか。
f　へびは なんびき いますか。

パズル 2

Tom's class has just conducted a pet survey. Listen carefully to Naomi to find out how many pets each classmate has and what they are. Then connect the appropriate names, numbers and pets from the lists below to show the information you have found out.

Tom •   • cat •   • 1
Kate •   • dog •   • 2
Sam •   • goat •   • 3
Miki •   • rabbit •   • 4
Ken •   • mouse •   • 5
Naomi •   • sheep •   • 6

mirai 2

いろいろな いろ

The names of the colours

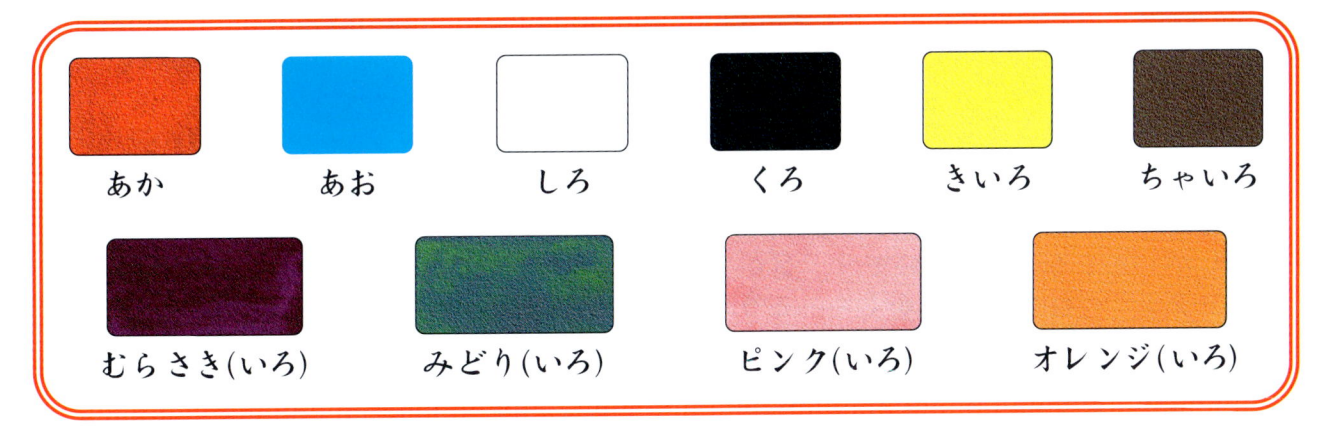

あか	あお	しろ	くろ	きいろ	ちゃいろ
むらさき(いろ)	みどり(いろ)	ピンク(いろ)	オレンジ(いろ)		

Using colours as adjectives

Some colours have an adjectival form. The table below shows you which of the colours have an adjectival form and the highlighted words indicate which expressions are used more commonly. The word いろ means *colour* and is optional for many colours.

To describe items by putting the colour in front of the item, as in *A red T-shirt*, either join the name of the colour to the item with particle の or use the adjectival form of the colour. So, in this case, you can say あかの T-シャツ or あかい T-シャツ.

You can also say *The T-shirt is red* using either the name of the colour or its adjectival form.

T-シャツは あかです or T-シャツは あかいです.

	Name of the colour + の	Adjectival form
red	あか＋の	あかい
white	しろ＋の	しろい
blue	あお＋の	あおい
black	くろ＋の	くろい
yellow	きいろ＋の	きいろい
brown	ちゃいろ＋の	ちゃいろい
purple	むらさき(いろ)＋の	
green	みどり(いろ)＋の	
pink	ピンク(いろ)＋の	
orange	オレンジ(いろ)＋の	

What's their favourite colour?

Which colours do Akira, Moe and Naomi like and which do they dislike? Listen carefully and complete the survey.

Name	Likes	Dislikes
あきら		
もえ		
なおみ		

part 2 • unit 5

67

日本からの Eメール

Email accessing mailbox...

こんにちは。おげんきですか。日よう日に わたしと おばは いのかしら こうえんに いきました。いのかしら こうえんは とうきょうに あります。とても きれいな こうえんです。かわや いろいろな 木や かだんや いけが あります。

おばの うちは いぬが います。いぬの なまえは パンダです。パンダは あしが とても みじかいです。目が おおきいです。日よう日に おばは いつも パンダを つれて、いのかしら こうえんへ いきます。パンダは こうえんが 大好きです。

おばの ともだちの うえださんと うちやまさんも ペットが います。うえださんは うさぎが います。そして、うちやまさんの うちは へんな ペットが います。しろいたちです。しろいたちは からだが ながいです。あしが みじかいです。そして、しっぽは とても ながいです。うえださんも うちやまさんも しゅうまつに ペットを つれて こうえんに いきます。でも、しろいたちは うさぎを たべます。だから、うえださんは 土よう日に、うちやまさんは 日よう日に こうえんに いきます。

さよなら。
ゆかり

Did you understand everything? **つれて** means *to take along with you*.

Inokashira Park is in a suburb of Tokyo called Mitaka. It is a very pretty park and is well known to Tokyo residents, so fine weekends can be very busy. People go to the park for all kinds of reasons. Band members go to practise; public speakers go to rehearse speeches; buskers play all kinds of instruments; artists paint the changing seasons; puppet-makers demonstrate their puppets; children play in the playgrounds; and people of all ages feed the waterbirds and take boats out onto the lake.

うちやまさんと しろいたちです。おもしろい ペットですね。ながい しっぽと みじかい あしが みえますか。しろいたちは うさぎが 大好きです。

The ferret's long body, long tail and short legs enable it to go down rabbit burrows to catch rabbits.

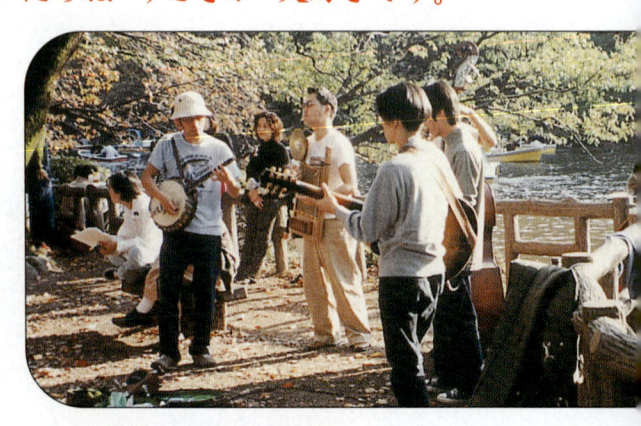

いのかしら こうえん

Did you know that insect pets are very popular in Japan? In the past people would travel to the countryside to catch fireflies and other insects as well as to enjoy listening to the singing insects while they were there. These insects are, for Japanese, the sounds of summer.

These days many kinds of singing insects such as crickets and katydids are kept in attractive bamboo cages designed as little houses and boats. Some look like portable radios. There is even an insect zoo called Toma Zoo near Tokyo and many department stores stock insect food and terrariums.

こどもたちは この むしが 大好きです。

Beetles are also very popular. Most families have a family member who has kept a rhinoceros or stag beetle at some time or other. Department stores stock beetle products to help pet owners to care successfully for their beetle pets. Beetle owners have little trouble finding such things as packets of decayed wood flakes for egg laying and beetle food made from wood sap! There are many companies that specialise in the production of beetle-related products.

はなこは かわいい ようふくが 大好き

かみのけ

きんぱつ　しらが　あかげ　カーリーヘア

て
あたま
め
みみ
かお ｛ はな
くち
かた
むね
け
うで
おなか
おしり
あし

Hanako loves to dress up in bright clothes and mess around. Look at her picture with all the parts of her body labelled and then do the activities below.

1 Are the following true or false?

はなこは 口が おおきいです。＿＿＿＿
はなこは うでが みじかいです。＿＿＿＿
はなこは あしが ながいです。＿＿＿＿
はなこは 目が 小さいです。＿＿＿＿
はなこは ドレスを きています。＿＿＿＿

2 Describe Hanako in three different ways.

3 Work in pairs as Kappa and Tengu.

Kappa: Choose a person both of you know. Describe the person to Tengu in five different ways.
Tengu: Guess whom Kappa is describing. Ask as many questions as you like.

やってみよう

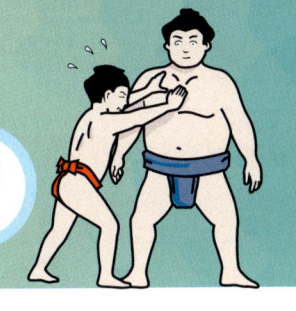

1 Has anybody found a dog?

The following people have lost their dogs! They are calling the dog pound and asking if anybody has handed them in. Listen to the conversation and write the appropriate letter in the brackets. If the pound does not have their dog, put a cross in the bracket.

1 Kate (　　)

2 Hiro (　　)

3 Shingo (　　)

4 Naomi (　　)

(a) (b) (c) (d) (e) (f)

2 Alien alert!

Tengu: You were just playing a computer game at home when, all of a sudden, the game disappeared and a funny thing happened. An alien appeared on your screen. You quickly grabbed the mobile phone and rang Kappa, who is an alien expert. Describe what you saw in detail to Kappa, answering any questions Kappa may have.

Kappa: You are an alien expert. You often receive information from witnesses about strange flying objects and aliens. You receive a phone call from Tengu today telling you about an alien that suddenly appeared on a computer screen. Ask Tengu for all the information you need to complete a detailed description. Draw what Tengu describes to you in order to keep it in your file. (Use your exercise book to draw in.)

Take turns.

Example:

てんぐ: もしもし。てんぐです。かっぱさん／くんですか。
かっぱ: はい。そうです。
てんぐ: いま、**alien** を みました。
かっぱ: どんな かおでしたか。

part 2　unit 5

3 トムくんは かみが むらさきいろです

Tengu: You have just started a rock band with a group of friends. Before starting the activity, label the picture above with the names of the rock band members. Use the eight names shown here.

| 1 Tom | 2 Poppy | 3 Kenny | 4 Miki |
| 5 Maki | 6 Kyle | 7 John | 8 Peter |

Kappa: Find out who is in Tengu's rock band by asking Tengu questions. Label the people in the picture with the number of their name.

Example:

かっぱ: トムくんは どれですか。

てんぐ: トムくんは 目があおいです。かみが むらさきいろです。くちが 小さいです。

4 Pet monitors

Nikki and Shinichi are class monitors in charge of the school pets. They have to count all the animals every day. Listen to their conversation and check if all the animals are there.

a Fill in the blank column in the chart.

b Are there any fewer or more animals than usual? Which ones?

	Usual number	Today's number
Fish	20	
Tortoises	5	
Frogs (red eyes)	8	
Frogs (yellow eyes)	10	
Sheep	9	
Rabbits	2	

mirai 2

5 なにいろの T-シャツが 好きですか

Tengu: Ask Kappa to choose three T-shirts in colours s/he particularly likes.
Add up the score of those three T-shirts to find out what kind of person Kappa is.
For example: なにいろの T-シャツが 好きですか。

Kappa: Choose three T-shirts in colours you like, then answer Tengu's question.
For example: あかい T-シャツと、あおい T-シャツと、むらさきの T-シャツが好きです。

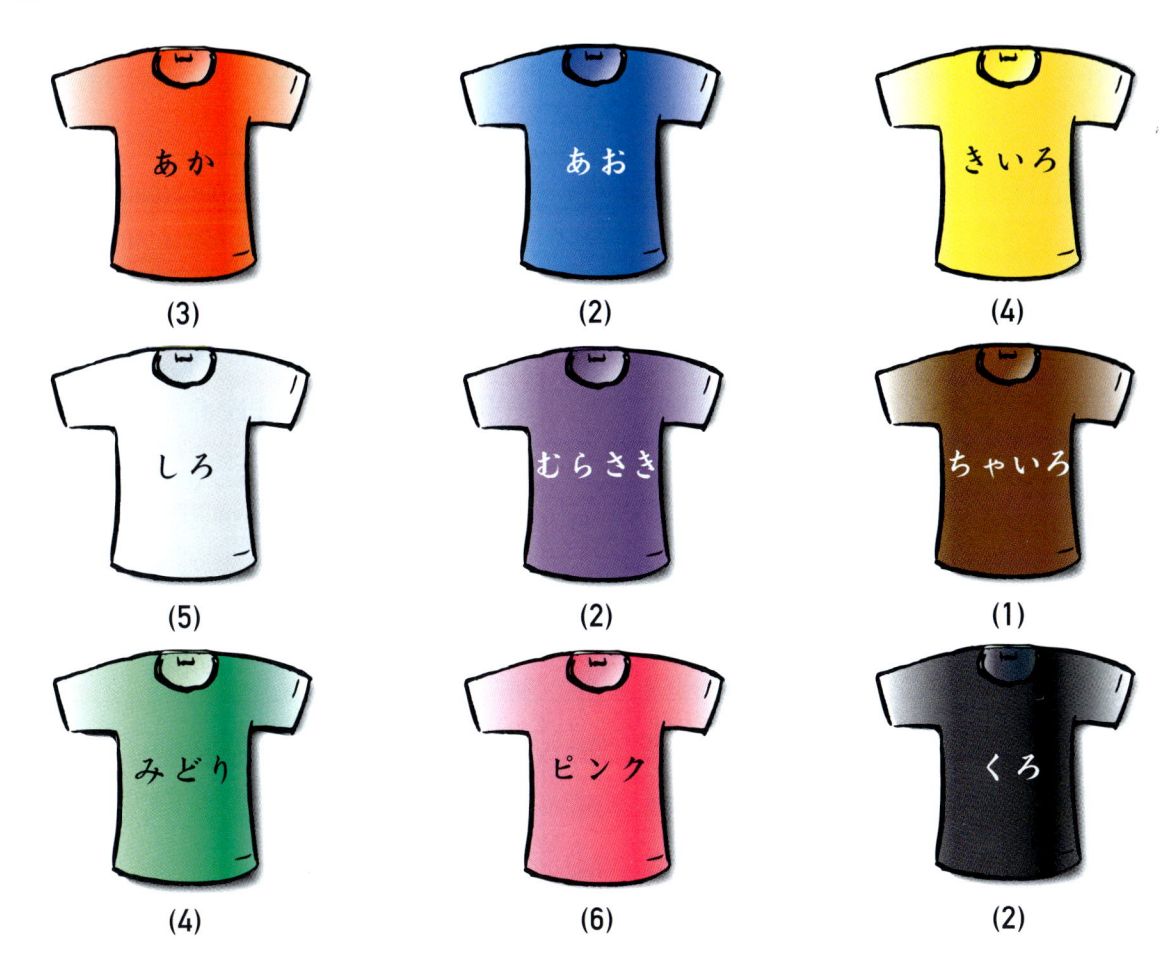

あか (3)　　あお (2)　　きいろ (4)

しろ (5)　　むらさき (2)　　ちゃいろ (1)

みどり (4)　　ピンク (6)　　くろ (2)

Score	Character traits
15–12	やさしい 人です。かわいい ペットが 好きですね。でも、ねずみは きらいですね。ともだちが たくさん いますね。ラッキーナンバーは 五と 九と 一です。
11–8	しんせつな 人です。パーティーが 大好きですね。らいしゅうの テストは むずかしいです。でも、だいじょうぶ。よくできます。ラッキーナンバーは 八と 二と 四です。
7–4	あたまがいい 人です。スポーツと えいがが 好きですね。かっこいい／きれいな 人と デートの チャンスが あります。ラッキーナンバーは 三と 六と 七です。

part 2 • unit 5

やった！

Commenting on particular things near to the speaker Commenting on particular things near to the listener Commenting on particular things at a distance from both speakers			この その あの	[thing]	は	[comment]	です。
Describing parts of a whole	A	[The whole]	は	[the part]	が	[description]	です。
	B	[The whole]	の	[the part]	は	[description]	です。
Asking someone to say the colour of something			なにいろ	の	[thing]		ですか。
Saying the colour of something							
あか、しろ、あお、くろ、きいろ、ちゃいろ			[Colour]	い	[thing]		です。
		or	[Colour]	の	[thing]		です。
			[Thing]	は	[colour]		です。
		or	[Thing]	は	[colour] い		です。
オレンジ(いろ)、ピンク(いろ)、むらさき(いろ)、みどり(いろ)			[Colour]	の	[thing]		です。
			[Thing]	は	[colour]		です。
Asking how many animals there are/someone has			[Animal]	は	なんびき		いますか。
Answering			[Animal]	は	[number] びき ひき びき ぴき		います。

漢字　かんじ

One way of remembering

口　くち　mouth

Where would we be without a mouth? No eating, no speaking, no kissing ...?

目　め　eye, eyes

Turn it on its side to see it!

カタカナ

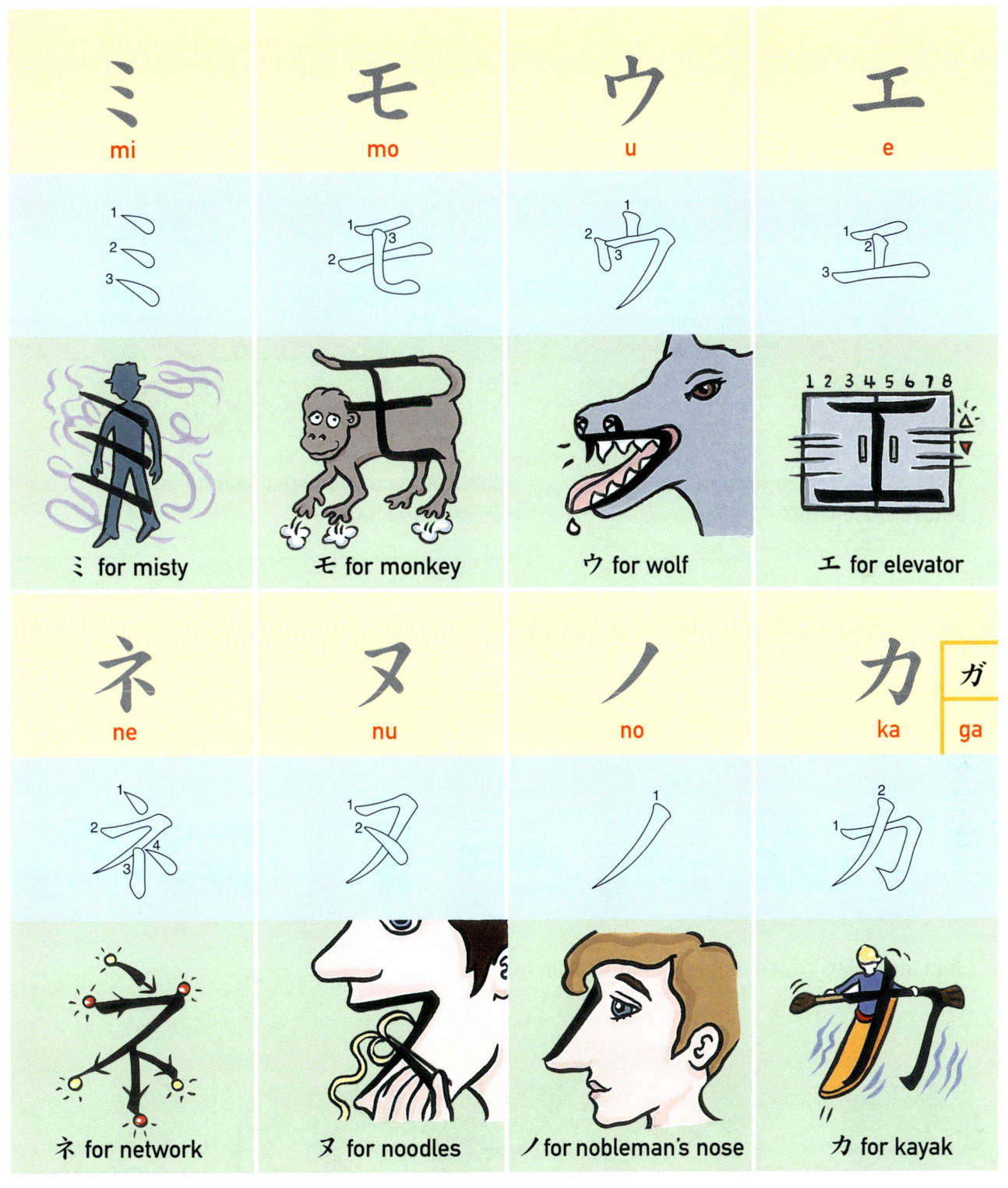

ミ mi	モ mo	ウ u	エ e
ミ for misty	モ for monkey	ウ for wolf	エ for elevator

ネ ne	ヌ nu	ノ no	カ ka / ガ ga
ネ for network	ヌ for noodles	ノ for nobleman's nose	カ for kayak

ン	ワ	ラ	ヤ	マ	ハ	ナ	タ	サ	カ	ア
	リ			ミ	ヒ	ニ	チ	シ	キ	イ
	ル	ユ		ム	フ	ヌ	ツ	ス	ク	ウ
	レ			メ	ヘ	ネ	テ	セ	ケ	エ
	ロ		ヨ	モ	ホ	ノ	ト	ソ	コ	オ

part 2 • unit 5

カタカナ れんしゅう

1 Find the following words in each of the grids and cross them out.

pink
orange
green

カ	ー	ピ	リ
オ	レ	ン	ジ
ー	ヘ	ク	ア
グ	リ	ー	ン

toilet
curry
lemon
monorail
noodle
Ed

エ	ド	レ	モ
ト	イ	レ	ノ
イ	オ	カ	レ
ン	ス	カ	ー
ヌ	ー	ド	ル
			ク

What word can you spell using the leftover katakana?

_____

What words can you spell using the leftover katakana?

_____ and _____

2 Link the countries' names with their flags.

カナダ   フランス   アメリカ   オーストラリア   スペイン   ブラジル   タイ

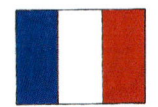

3 Join these Australian animals' names with their pictures.

コアラ   カンガルー   ウォンバット   エミュー   ディンゴ

4 The syllables of this katakana word are jumbled up. Put them in the correct order to spell 'navy blue'.

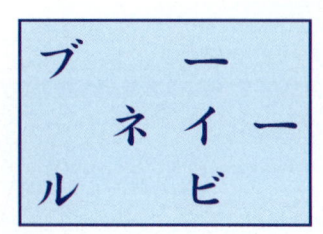

ブ ー
ネ イ
ル ビ

76   mirai 2

チェック しましょう!

Body parts

あし	foot and leg
あたま	head
うで	arm
(お)しり	bottom, hips
おなか	stomach
かお	face
かた	shoulder(s)
かみ	hair
からだ	body

け	animal hair
口(くち)	mouth
しっぽ	tail
て	hand
はな	nose
みみ	ear(s)
目(め)	eye(s)
むね	chest

Colours

あお	blue
あか	red
いろ	colour
オレンジ(いろ)	orange
きいろ	yellow
くろ	black

しろ	white
ちゃいろ	brown
ピンク(いろ)	pink
みどり(いろ)	green
むらさき(いろ)	purple

Creatures

か	mosquito
かえる	frog
しろいたち	ferret
はえ	fly
ひきがえる	cane toad
ひつじ	sheep
むし	insect
やぎ	goat
わらいかわせみ	kookaburra

Adjectives

いや(な)	horrible, nasty
いろいろ(な)	various
ながい	long
みじかい	short
みにくい	ugly

Verb

きます	wear shirt, dress

Expressions

それに	in addition, besides
など	and so on
～くらい or ぐらい	about, approximately
とても	awfully, very

Places

オーストラリア	Australia
みなみアメリカ	South America

Time words

むかし	long ago, in the past

Identifying words

あの～	that ～ over there
この～	this ～
その～	that ～

Hair

きんぱつ	blonde hair
しらが	grey, white hair
あかげ	red hair
カーリーヘア	curly hair

Question words

どの～	Which ～?
なんびき	How many animals?
なにいろ	What colour?

Other noun

どく	poison

Suffix

～ひき	counter for animals

I can:
- ○ ask how many pets someone has
- ○ say how many pets I have
- ○ describe others' pets as well as my own
- ○ describe people's appearance
- ○ understand descriptions of pets and people
- ○ read and write descriptions of pets and people
- ○ read and write 目 and 口.

part 2 • unit 5

Unit 6

あなの 中に なにが いますか

1.
- うちに あそびに きませんか。バーベキューを しましょう。
- 土よう日です。
- いつですか。

2.
- へえ！いいですね！でも、ニッキーさんの うちは どこに ありますか。
- とおいですよ。ニッキーさんの うちは いなかに あります。父の くるまで いっしょに いきましょうか。

3.
- はい、おねがいします。
- のみものは れいぞうこの 中に あります。どうぞ、ステーキや ソーセージは あそこに あります。

4.
- ごちそうさま。
- おいしかったです。

5.
- ニッキーさん、きて ください。木の 下に へんな あなが あります。
- うわー！ほんとう。大きい あなですね。きをつけて！てを いれては だめです。

78　mirai 2

6

あなの 中に なにが いますか。
へびですか。

いいえ、へび じゃないですよ。
もっと、大きい どうぶつです。

7

コアラですか。

いいえ、コアラは 木の
上に います。

あ！

8

よるまで
まちましょう。

9

わあ、かわいい！！

すごい！ウォンバットです。

やってみよう
さがして ください

* the words for *inside the refrigerator*
* how to say *Yes please, thank you*
* how to say *There is a strange hole*
* the words for *under the tree* and *up in the tree*
* the words for *in the country*
* how to say *It's a bigger animal*
* how to say *Won't you come and have fun at my house?*
* how to say *You shouldn't put your hand in*
* the word for *over there*.

part 2 • unit 6

あきのやまに ききましょう

Why does Nikki say きませんか instead of きて ください?

She says this because she wants it to sound more like a request than a command. It is similar to *Wouldn't you like to come?* うちに あそびに きませんか is how we invite someone to come and have fun at our place. あそびます changes to あそびに to show that the reason for the invitation is *to have fun*. You will learn more about this on page 82.

When do you use おねがいします?

おねがいします is a very useful expression. Use it when someone asks if they can do something for you and you agree. It is the equivalent of saying *I'd like you to do that for me, please* or *Yes please, thank you*.

If あそこ means *over there*, how do you say *here*, *there* and *where*?

The words for *here*, *there*, *over there* and *where* start with the same syllables as words you already know: これ、それ、あれ and どれ; and この、その、あの and どの. They are: ここ (*here*) そこ (*there*) あそこ (*over there*) and どこ (*where?*). Look on page 82 to find out more.

By the way, this unit introduces some more precise words to describe where things are. You have already met 中 (なか) meaning *inside*, 上 (うえ) meaning *up in* and 下 (した) meaning *under*. Keep a lookout for others on page 83! The kanji give clues to the meaning. You can see how on page 91.

What does てを いれては だめです mean?

It means *You shouldn't put your hand inside*. いれます means *put in*. When the end of a verb is 〜ては だめです the meaning is to warn someone not to do something. It literally means *If you do this it is not good*. You will find more about how to use this phrase on page 86.

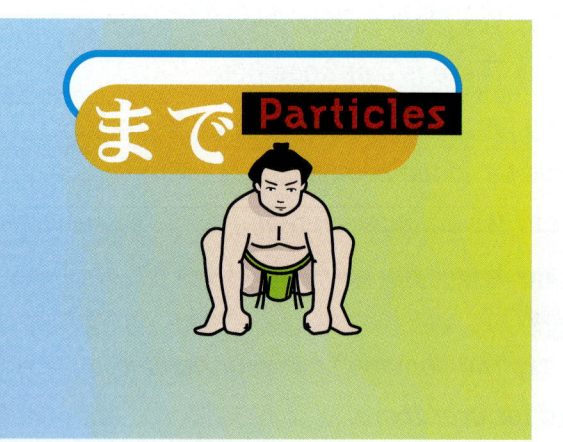

まで Particles

The word まで, meaning *until* or *as far as*, is another particle. It can occur by itself after a time word or after a place. It is often used with から (*from*).

Time word → まで → verb

Place → まで → verb of movement

mirai 2

がんばれ

Saying the purpose for going/coming somewhere

こうえんへ あそびに いきます／きます。
I am going to the park to have fun.

まちへ えいがを みに いきます。
I am going to town to see a movie.

ひろくんは おんがくを ききに きました。
Hiro came to listen to music.

Saying where animals or people are

ねこは きの うえに います。
The cat is up in the tree.

おとこのこは ベッドの したに います。
The boy is under the bed.

きの うえに ねこが います。
There is a cat up in the tree.

ベッドの したに おとこのこが います。
There is a boy under the bed.

Saying where things are

えんぴつは かばんの なかに あります。
The pencil is inside the bag.

かばんの なかに えんぴつが あります。
There is a pencil inside the bag.

Advising someone not to do something

あなの なかに てを いれては だめです。
Don't put your hand in the hole.

ここで すいえいを しては だめです。
Don't swim here.

Saying until when someone does something

10じまで べんきょう します。
I will study until 10 o'clock.

ひろくんは 7じから 9じまで はたらきました。
Hiro worked from 7 until 9 o'clock.

Saying how far someone or something goes or comes

なおみさんは がっこうまで あるきました。
Naomi walked as far as the school.

ニッキーさんは バスで がっこうから まちまで いきました。
Nikki went by bus from school to town.

part 2 • unit 6

ここ、そこ、あそこ

ねこは どこですか

- ねこは どこですか。 ここです。
- ねこは どこですか。 ねこは あそこです。
- ねこは どこですか。 そこです。

The question could be phrased like this: ねこは どこに いますか. In this case, the replies would be:
- ここに います or
- そこに います or
- あそこに います.

Remember that particle に is needed after position words if you use います or あります.

まちへ なにを しに いきますか
What are you going to town to do?

- まちへ なにを しに いきますか。
- かいものを しに いきます。
- ペット ショーを みに いきます。
- ペット ショー 1じから
- こうえんへ あそびに いきます。
- コンサートを ききに いきます。

82 mirai 2

あきらくんは どこに いますか

Study the drawing and then answer the following questions.

1 テレビの うしろに なにが いますか。
2 ほんだなの 中に なにが ありますか。
3 テーブルの 上に なにが ありますか。
4 いぬは どこに いますか。
5 スリッパは どこに ありますか。
6 あきらくんは どこに いますか。

part 2 • unit 6

日本からの Eメール

Email — accessing mailbox...

　こんにちは。おげんきですか。せんしゅう、わたしは かぞくと きゅうしゅうへ いきました。きゅうしゅうは おんせんが たくさん あります。わたしたちは おんせんが 大好きです。わたしたちは べっぷに とまりました。べっぷの ちかくに ゆうめいな こくりつこうえんが あります。たかさきやまです。たかさきやまは かざんです。むかし ふんかしました。でも、いまは、しずかです。

　たかさきやまには さるが たくさん います。わたしは おとうと 二人で さるを みに いきました。たかさきやまの さるは おりの 中に いません。やまの 中に じゆうに すんで います。だから とても げんきです。わたしたちは やまの 上まで のぼりました。木の 上に さるを 10ぴき みました。その さるは かおが あかかったです。しっぽが ながかったです。とても 小さい さるも 1ぴき みました。お母さんの せなかに いました。わたしたちは しゃしんを たくさん とりました。

　それから、やまを おりました。さるの ばんごはんは 5じに はじまりました。さるは 100ぴきぐらい たべものを たべに きました。さるは バナナや りんごや オレンジが 大好きです。とても おもしろかったです。オーストラリアには さるが いますか。

　　　　　　　　　　　　　　　　　　おへんじを まって います。
　　　　　　　　　　　　　　　　　　　　　　　　　　　ゆかり

Did you manage to understand all of that? Japan has lots of national parks (こくりつ こうえん) but Mt Takasaki National Park at the western end of the city of Oita is famous for the hundreds of macaque monkeys that live there. The mountain is not really a mountain but a dormant volcano. The kanji for volcano is 火山 (かざん), which means fire mountain, a good word for a volcano don't you think?

It must have been impressive long ago when a huge sea of larva flowed down the slopes into the sea.

My brother and I went to see the monkeys by ourselves. 二人で (ふたりで) means the two of us together. If you do something alone you can say 一人で (ひとりで). We climbed (のぼりました) to the top of the mountain following the walking tracks. We saw lots of monkeys going up, but even more when we came down (おりました) to the feeding grounds at the bottom. It was an amazing sight. Monkeys arrived in groups of about a hundred to feed together. I took lots of photos (しゃしんを たくさん とりました) and I'll send you some soon.

　Please write and tell me about the wildlife in your country. I look forward to receiving your message.

84　　　mirai 2

We stayed (とまりました) in Beppu, which is near (ちかくに) Mt Takasaki. At Beppu there are many famous sites, such as boiling pools and a geyser as well as hot sands. We stayed there because of the hot springs (おんせん). All my family love to bathe in the naturally hot water of the springs. One of the hotels has particularly huge hot spring baths. These are very popular because they are as big as swimming pools, have a jungle of plants growing all around and slides into the water.

We bathe in a hot spring bath in the same way we do at home. Everyone washes outside the bath sitting on small stools, using taps set along the wall or showers. Then we relax in the hot steamy water. Of course we don't wear bathers or take washers into the pool, because it really is a bath not a swimming pool. In case you are wondering, there are separate baths for males and females!

Monkeys live in other parts of Japan too. They used to be everywhere, but in recent times they have retreated to the mountain regions. In fact, some Japanese monkeys are the most northerly living monkeys in the world. In the winter, many feet of snow fall and the mountains are extremely cold. The monkeys are exceptionally clever and have devised a way of surviving in the freezing conditions. No one knows how long they have been doing it, but troupes of monkeys have been filmed and photographed making their way down the snowy slopes to natural hot springs which occur all through the mountains. At the hot springs the animals climb into the steaming water and sit up to their necks in it keeping warm.

てを いれては だめです

You probably remember how to ask permission to do something using the form 〜も いいですか. The way to warn someone that they shouldn't do something is quite similar.

Just replace 〜も いいですか with 〜は だめです. For example:

May I open the window?	まど	を	あけて	も	いい	ですか。
You shouldn't open the window.	まど	を	あけて	は	だめ	です。

You use this form when in English you might say 'You shouldn't ...' or 'You'd better not ...'.

Now tell someone they shouldn't do something using some verbs you already know. Follow the example.

Example: みます → みて → みては だめです。

1 たべます → たべて → _____
2 はなします → はなして → _____
3 よみます → よんで → _____
4 はたらきます → はたらいて → _____
5 いきます → いって → _____
6 のみます → のんで → _____

ヘルシー ライフ スタイル Healthy lifestyle

Your family agreed to host a young Japanese exchange student, but he turned out to be rather naughty. The pictures below show some of the things that have most annoyed your family. It's up to you to tell him he shouldn't do them. Use the clues to help you. The first one has been done as an example.

…に ねます → …に ねて
12じに ねては だめです。
_____

…に おきます → …に おきて
1 _____

…を のみます → …を のんで
2 _____

まいにち …を たべます → まいにち …を たべて
3 _____

一人で …に いきます → 一人で …に いって
4 _____

ごちそうさまでした。おいしかったです。

AB p. 56(2), 65

In Unit 3 you learned how to describe things and the different ways of using い and な adjectives. Then, in Unit 4, you learned how to form the negative using these adjectives. Here you will find out how to describe how something or someone was in the past tense.

1 い adjectives

Simply drop off the final い and add かったです, like this:

すしは おいし~~い~~です + かったです。

Present tense	Past tense
きょう、とうきょうは あついです。 Tokyo is hot today.	きのう、とうきょうは あつかった です。 Tokyo was hot yesterday.
すずきせんせいは きびしいです。 Mr Suzuki is strict.	すずきせんせいは きびしかったです。 Mr Suzuki was strict.
ひろくんの いぬは 小さいです。 Hiro's dog is small.	ひろくんの いぬは 小さかったです。 Hiro's dog was small.

2 な adjectives

Simply add でした, like this:

ゆきさんは げんき~~です~~ + でした。

Present tense	Past tense
父は ゆうめいです。 My father is famous.	父は ゆうめいでした。 My father was famous.
いなかは しずかです。 The countryside is quiet.	いなかは しずかでした。 The countryside was quiet.
トムくんは しんせつです。 Tom is kind.	トムくんは しんせつでした。 Tom was kind.

3 い adjectives or な adjectives + noun です

Simply add でした to the noun, like this:

ぼくの いぬは かわいい いぬ~~です~~ + でした。
まちださんは きれいな 人~~です~~ + でした。

Present tense	Past tense
ケンさんは かっこいい 人です。 Ken is a cool guy.	ケンさんは かっこいい 人でした。 Ken was a cool guy.
ひるごはんは おいしい ピザです。 Lunch is a delicious pizza.	ひるごはんは おいしい ピザでした。 Lunch was a delicious pizza.
この まちは しずかな まちです。 This town is a quiet town.	この まちは しずかな まちでした。 This town was a quiet town.
そふは ゆうめいな 人です。 My grandfather is a famous person.	そふは ゆうめいな 人でした。 My grandfather was a famous person.

part 2 • unit 6

やってみよう

1 しゅうまつは どうでしたか

Tengu: You have been very busy this weekend and now you can't wait to tell Kappa all about it. Decide what you did over the weekend by choosing a word from each band in the chart below. Prepare five sentences by joining these words with suitable particles to tell Kappa what you did and how it was.

Kappa: Unfortunately, you had to stay in this weekend and weren't able to join in with Tengu's plans. Now you want to know all about it. First ask what Tengu did and then ask how it was. Get Tengu to tell you about five different things.

Your conversation might begin something like this. You will have to supply all the words in black!

かっぱ: しゅうまつは あつかったですね。なにを しましたか。
てんぐ: ともだちと、やきとりを たべに いきました。
かっぱ: やきとりは どうでしたか。
てんぐ: とても おいしかったです。

Take turns.

ともだち	やきとり		まあまあ
母	すし	たべに	きれい
父	ハンバーガー		おいしい
兄	コンサート	かいに	おもしろい
いもうと	えいが		つまらない
あね	おんがく	ききに	まずい
おとうと	T-シャツ		たのしい
	ほん		いい
	シーディー	みに	へん

いきました。

mirai 2

2 Find the secret word

Listen carefully to the clues to choose the right katakana from the picture.
Put the syllables in the right order in the boxes to find the secret words.

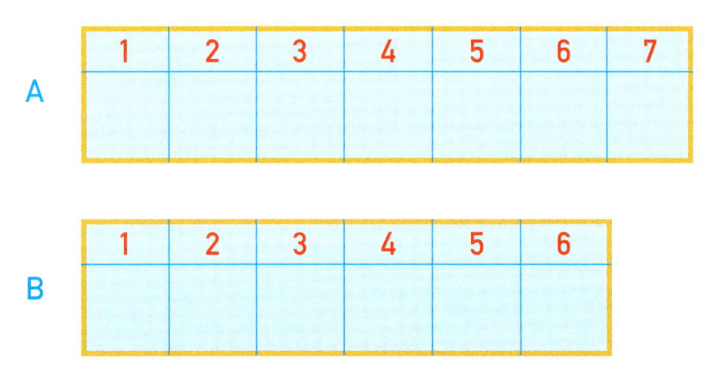

	1	2	3	4	5	6	7
A							

	1	2	3	4	5	6
B						

3 かくれんぼ (Hide and seek)

Tengu: Use your magic powers to shrink and hide yourself in the picture.
Write in your notebook where you are.

Kappa: Find out where Tengu is by guessing instead of asking directly.

For example: てんぐさんは いすの 下に いますか。

Keep asking questions until you find Tengu, then change roles.

part 2 • unit 6

4 なんじから なんじまで ですか

Kappa: Imagine you have a holiday job working for the Customer Service Department of Animal Park. Your job is to answer phone enquiries. First fill out the timetable, then get ready to answer Tengu's questions. Make sure you answer in Japanese!

Tengu: Imagine you are a Japanese tourist and you have been told about a great place to go: Animal Park. You need to phone up and ask what times the park is open and when you are allowed to take photos of the koalas. You especially don't want to miss the snake show! The hints below the timetable should give you some ideas.

Animal Park

OPENING HOURS
Mon–Fri _____ ~ _____
Sat _____ ~ _____
Sun _____ ~ _____

SNAKE SHOW
_____ ~ _____

KOALA PHOTO TIME
_____ ~ _____

Hints:

〜ようびは なんじから なんじまでですか。

コアラの しゃしんの じかんは なんじから なんじまでですか。

へびの ショーは なんじから なんじまでですか。

---

5 What have they been up to?

Nikki's school has been hosting some Japanese exchange students for the past two weeks. Her teacher is curious about how they spent their weekends with their host families. Listen to the conversation and help her to fill in the information in the chart in English.

	Places	Purposes	Their opinion
1	Department store		
2		To eat pizza	
3			
4			

やった！

Saying the purpose for coming or going	[Place]	へ/に	[verb]~~ます~~	に	いきます/きます。		
Saying where people/animals are	[Person/animal]	は	[place]	の	[position]	に		います。
	or		[Place]	の	[position]	に	[person/animal] が	
Saying where things are	[Thing]	は	[place]	の	[position]	に		あります。
	or		[Place]	の	[position]	に	[thing] が	
Advising someone not to do something	[Verb]	て	は	だめ	です。			
Saying until when someone does something	[Time]	まで	[verb].					
	[Time]	から	[time] まで [verb].					
Saying how far someone goes or comes	[Place]	まで	[verb of movement].					
	[Place]	から	[place] まで [verb of movement].					

漢字　かんじ

One way of remembering

上　うえ　up, above

Imagine a caterpillar standing upright on a leaf, looking up above for somewhere to climb.

下　した　down, below

Here the caterpillar hangs down below the leaf, looking for tasty morsels.

中　なか　ちゅう　middle, inside

Imagine an arrow in the middle of a target, having passed right through the inside!

part 2 • unit 6

カタカナ

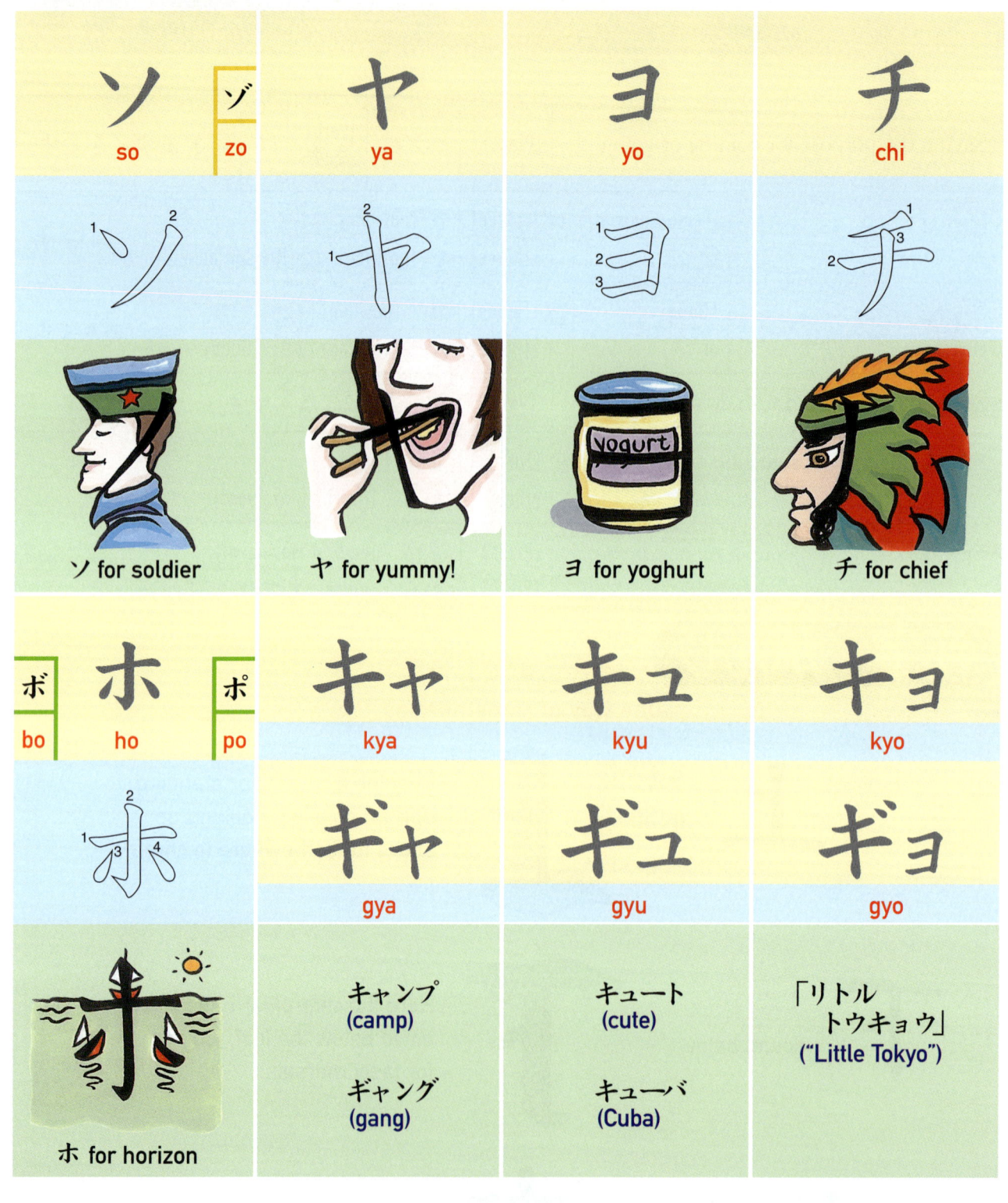

ソ so / ゾ zo	ヤ ya	ヨ yo	チ chi
ソ for soldier	ヤ for yummy!	ヨ for yoghurt	チ for chief
ホ ho / ボ bo / ポ po	キャ kya	キュ kyu	キョ kyo
	ギャ gya	ギュ gyu	ギョ gyo
ホ for horizon	キャンプ (camp) / ギャング (gang)	キュート (cute) / キューバ (Cuba)	「リトル トウキョウ」 ("Little Tokyo")

ン ワ ラ ヤ マ ハ ナ タ サ カ ア
　 リ 　 ミ ヒ ニ チ シ キ イ
　 ル ユ ム フ ヌ ツ ス ク ウ
　 レ 　 メ ヘ ネ テ セ ケ エ
　 ロ ヨ モ ホ ノ ト ソ コ オ

92　mirai 2

カタカナ　れんしゅう

AB p. 59

1　カタカナ　クロスワード

Fill in the crossword in English using the katakana clues.

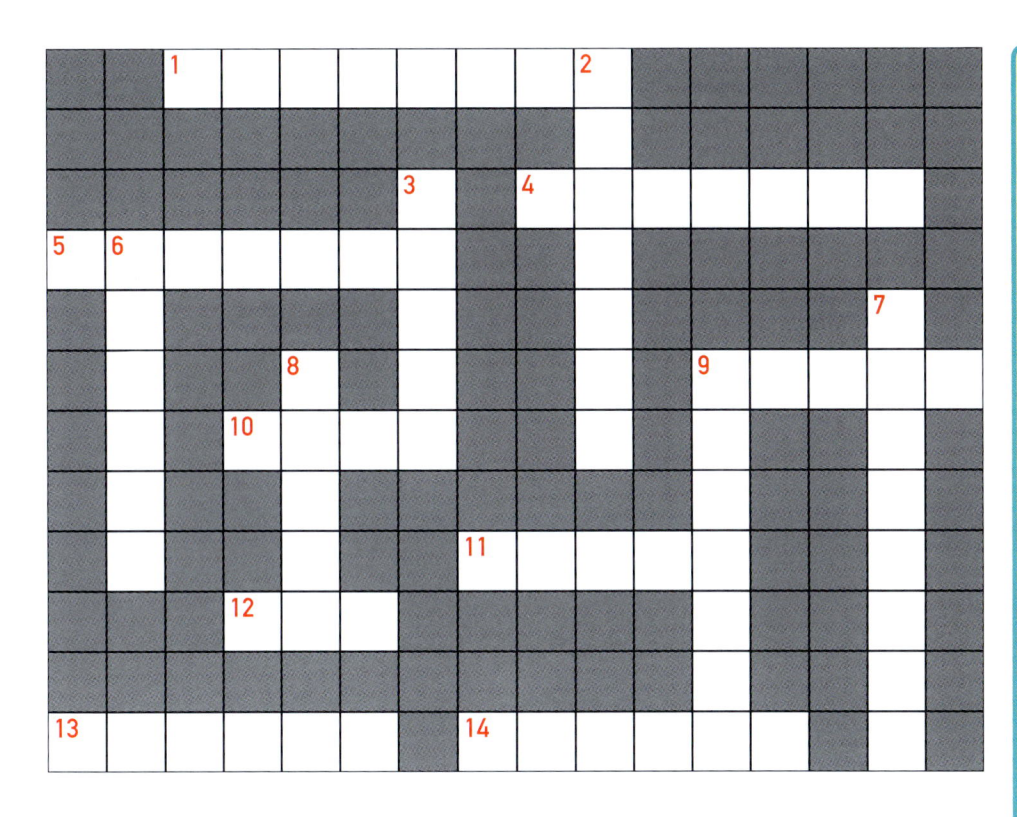

Across
1　アイスクリーム
4　ラザーニヤ
5　ヨーグルト
9　サラダ
10　ミルク
11　チップス
12　ハム
13　トマト
14　コーヒー

Down
2　ミートパイ
3　ステーキ
6　オレンジ
7　サンドイッチ
8　ピザ
9　ソーセージ

2　Find the following wild animals in the field below and label them.

パンダ　　チンパンジー　　ビーバー　　ゴリラ　　ピューマ

part 2 • unit 6

93

チェック しましょう！

Expressions
おねがいします	Yes, please
たくさん	a lot, many
もっと	more
もっと 大きい	bigger
一人で (ひとりで)	alone, by myself
二人で (ふたりで)	together, the two of us

Nouns
あな	hole
おんせん	hot spring
おり	cage
き	tree
しゃしん	photograph
ステーキ	steak
ソーセージ	sausage(s)
のみもの	drink
バーベキュー	BBQ
りんご	apple
れいぞうこ	refrigerator

Position words
上 (うえ)	up, above
うしろ	behind
下 (した)	down, below
そば	on the side of
ちかくに	close to
中 (なか)	inside
まえ	in front

Animals
ウォンバット	wombat
コアラ	koala
さる	monkey

Time words
しゅうまつ	weekend
よる	night, night-time

Places
いなか	countryside
かざん	volcano
こくりつこうえん	national park

Adjectives
おいしかったです	was delicious
とおい	far away

Verbs
おります	go down
とまります	stay, stop at
とります	take
のぼります	go up, climb
のみます	drink
ふんかします	erupt
まちます	wait

Adverb
じゆうに	freely

I can:
○ agree to an offer of help
○ invite someone to my house
○ describe things in the past
○ say more precisely where things, people and animals are
○ answer questions about where things, people and animals are
○ advise someone not to do six things
○ read and write about animals
○ read and write 上, 下 and 中
○ read and write all katakana words.

94　　　mirai 2

part 3

Let's have fun!

At the end of Part 3 you will be able to talk and write about:

- what you want to do and don't want to do
- the weather
- eating and ordering food in a restaurant
- the seasons
- shopping
- dates and birthdays.

You will also find out more about Japan and learn some more kanji and katakana.

あそびに いきましょう

Unit 7 スキーに いきたい

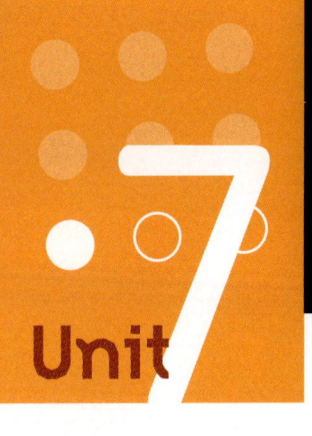

1. しゅうまつは なにを しますか。
ぼくは えいがが 見たいです。
おもしろい えいがが ありますか。

はい、らいしゅう、「てんせい」が はじまりますよ。しんぶんで 見ました。

2. わたしは えいがは 見たくないです。
いっしょに スケートに いきませんか。

わたしは スケートが できません。

3. せんしゅう、山に ゆきが たくさん ふりましたね。スキーは どうですか。

4. いいですね。スキーに いきたいです。

5. ええーっ！スキー？ ぼく、スキーは はじめてです。むずかしいですか。

いいえ、ぜんぜん むずかしくないですよ。

6 だいじょうぶです。ゆうめいな スキーの インストラクターが います。日本人です。父の ともだちです。

7 うわーっ！きもちがいい！！
いい てんきですねえ。
さむいですよ。

8 わたしの ように あるいて ください。

9 うわあ！たすけて！

10 まさしくんは どこ？

11 スキーは よかったですね。
スキーは よく なかったですよ。

やってみよう
さがして ください

* a word that means *want to see*
* words that mean *I saw it in the paper*
* a word that means *don't want to see*
* words that mean *I want to go skiing*
* a word that means *Help!*
* the words for *good weather*
* an expression that means *a great feeling*
* words that mean *lots of snow fell*
* an expression that means *It's the first time*
* how to say *It wasn't good.*

part 2 • unit 7

あきのやまに ききましょう

Can you put たい after any verb to mean *want to*?

You can add it to any verb where it makes sense. Just replace the ます ending with たいです。

The particle used with 〜たい is へ if you want to go somewhere. If you want to say something that usually takes the object particle を you can use either を or が. For example, some people say えいがを みたいです. Others say えいがが みたいです. I expect there are ways of saying things in English that vary according to the speaker. Can you think of any? If you want to find out more about using 〜たい see page 100.

How do you say you *don't* want to do something?

たい changes in the same way that い adjectives do, so to say *don't want to*, change たいです to たくないです. You usually use the particle は. For example: えいがは みたくないです.

Does よくなかったです mean *it wasn't good*?

Yes, that's right. As you know, the past form of いい is よかった. This is because the word for 'good' used to be よい. So, the present negative of いい is よくないです and the past is よくなかったです. You'll find more about making the past negative of adjectives on page 102.

What does はじめてです mean?

This is a useful expression which means *It is the first time (I have done this)*.

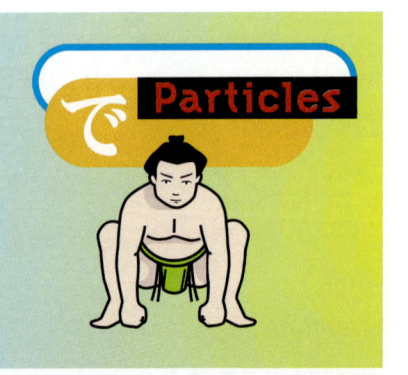

で Particles

You already know two uses of the particle で. One use is after a means of transport, as in でんしゃで いきます, where で has the basic meaning of *by* or *using*. The other use of で is after the place where some action occurs, as in こうえんで あそびます, where で means *in* or *at*. In this unit you will come across another use of で, in which it comes after an object that is *used*. In English you say 'I read it *in* the paper', 'I saw it *on* TV', 'I heard it *on* the radio' and so on. In Japanese, these ideas are all expressed with the particle で. You can think of it as meaning *using*.

mirai 2

がんばれ

Asking if someone wants to go somewhere
やま へ いきたいですか。
Do you want to go to the <u>mountains</u>?

Saying you want to go somewhere
うみへ いきたいです。
I want to go to the <u>sea</u>.

Saying you don't want to go somewhere; you want to go somewhere else
山へ(は) いきたくないです。うみへ いきたいです。
I don't want to go to the <u>mountains</u>. I want to go to the <u>sea</u>.

Asking if someone wants to do something
えいがが 見たいですか。
えいがを 見たいですか。
Do you want to <u>see</u> a <u>movie</u>?

Saying you want to do something
しんぶんが よみたいです。
しんぶんを よみたいです。
I want to <u>read</u> the <u>newspaper</u>.

Saying you don't want to do something; you want to do something else
えいがは 見たくないです。テニスが したいです。
I don't want to watch a movie. I want to play tennis.

Asking where someone obtained information
テレビで 見ましたか。
Did you see it on TV?

Saying where you obtained information
はい、テレビで 見ました。
Yes, I saw it on TV.
いいえ、しんぶんで よみました。
No, I read it in the paper.
いいえ、ラジオで ききました。
No, I heard it on the radio.

Asking about the weather
てんきは どうですか。
What is the weather like?

Commenting on the weather
いい てんきです。　はれです。
The weather is fine.　It is fine.
いやな てんきです。　くもりです。
The weather is unpleasant.　It is cloudy.
あめが ふって います。　ゆきが ふって います。
It is raining.　It is snowing.

Saying what the weather will probably be
はれ／あめ／くもり でしょう。
It will probably be fine/wet/cloudy.

part 3 • unit 7　99

テニスが したいです

The verb ending 〜たい changes in the same way as い adjectives to make the negative and the past tense.

	Present tense		Past tense	
	〜たいです (want to)	〜たくないです (don't want to)	〜たかったです (wanted to)	〜たくなかったです (didn't want to)
go	いきたいです	いきたくないです	いきたかったです	いきたくなかったです
eat	たべたいです	たべたくないです	たべたかったです	たべたくなかったです
see	みたいです	みたくないです	みたかったです	みたくなかったです
do/play	したいです	したくないです	したかったです	したくなかったです
listen	ききたいです	ききたくないです	ききたかったです	ききたくなかったです

Examples:

テニスが したいです or テニスを したいです。
I want to play tennis.
Notice the particle can be が or を.

テニスは したくないです。
I don't want to play tennis.
Notice the particle changes to は.

まちへ／に いきたかったです。
I wanted to go to town.

まちへは／には いきたくなかったです。
I didn't want to go to town.
Notice the particle は is added.

1 Decide which of the following activities you *want* to do and which you *don't* want to do. Change the sentences to reflect your wishes.
↳ Don't forget to change the particles where necessary.
  a 土よう日に えいがを みます。
  b 日よう日に うみへ いきます。
  c あした すしを たべます。
  d きょう いぬと あそびます。

2 Decide which of the following activities you *wanted* to do and which you *didn't* want to do. Change the sentences to reflect your wishes. Don't forget to change the particles.
  a きのう シーディーを ききました。
  b 金よう日に スキーを しました。
  c 月よう日に まちへ いきました。
  d きのう ピザを たべました。

In Japanese you can't say what others want to do using 〜たいです. If you want to express other people's wishes use 〜たい そうです.

For example:
ケンくんは えいがを みたい そうです。

やってみよう

1 Shipwrecked! You have been stranded on a desert island after a shipwreck! Write what you would most like to do in the bubbles.

2 Dream holiday

Tengu: Kappa will ask you questions to find out what your dream holiday would be. Secretly write down a favourite place from range 1, an activity from range 2, a time/day from range 3 and a person from range 4. Now answer Kappa's questions.

Kappa: You must find out Tengu's ideal holiday by asking questions in Japanese. Write down Tengu's answers in your exercise book.

For example:

かっぱ：アメリカへ　いきたいですか。
てんぐ：いいえ、アメリカへ　いきたくないです。
かっぱ：さっぽろへ　いきたいですか。
てんぐ：はい、いきたいです。

Where?	
To do what?	
When?	
With whom?	

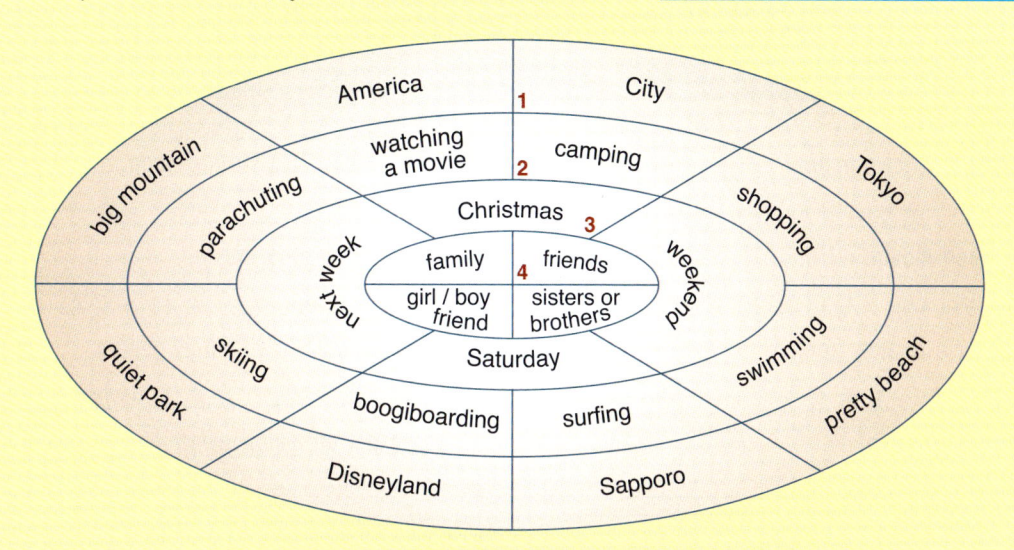

Range 1: America, City, Tokyo, pretty beach, Sapporo, Disneyland, quiet park, big mountain

Range 2: watching a movie, camping, shopping, swimming, surfing, boogiboarding, skiing, parachuting

Range 3: Christmas, weekend, Saturday, Disneyland, next week

Range 4: family, friends, sisters or brothers, girl / boy friend

part 3 • unit 7

スキーは たのしくなかったです

Saying something or someone *was not* ~ using い and な adjectives

1 い adjectives   Simply take off ない and add なかったです.

Example: スキーは たのしくないです + なかったです。

Present tense	Past tense
スケートは むずかしくないです。 Skating isn't difficult.	スケートは むずかしくなかったです。 Skating wasn't difficult.
その えいがは よくないです。 That movie isn't good.	その えいがは よくなかったです。 That movie wasn't good.
コーチは こわくないです。 The coach isn't scary.	コーチは こわくなかったです。 The coach wasn't scary.

2 な adjectives   Simply take off ない and add なかったです.

Example: たなかさんは しんせつじゃないです + なかったです。

Present tense	Past tense
ジムくんは げんきじゃないです。 Jim isn't well.	ジムくんは げんきじゃなかったです。 Jim wasn't well.
こうえんは しずかじゃないです。 The park isn't quiet.	こうえんは しずかじゃなかったです。 The park wasn't quiet.
いまは きれいじゃないです。 The living room isn't clean.	いまは きれいじゃなかったです。 The living room wasn't clean.

3 い or な adjective + noun ない です

Simply take off ない and add なかったです.
Example: スミスさんは いい人じゃないです + なかったです。
いずみさんは へんな 女の子じゃないです + なかったです。

Present tense	Past tense
父は きびしい 人じゃないです。 My father isn't a strict person.	父は きびしい 人じゃなかったです。 My father wasn't a strict person.
それは いい えいがじゃないです。 That isn't a good movie.	それは いい えいがじゃなかったです。 That wasn't a good movie.
母は ゆうめいな 人じゃないです。 My mother isn't a famous person.	母は ゆうめいな 人じゃなかったです。 My mother wasn't a famous person.
そこは いやな まちじゃないです。 That isn't an awful town.	そこは いやな まちじゃなかったです。 That wasn't an awful town.

やってみよう

1 やすみは どうでしたか

Yukari and Shingo have just come back from their holidays. Listen and write their impressions of the different activities they did in the bubbles. Write in English in your notebook.

For example: It was fun.

Additional vocabulary: およぎます swim

2 あした なにを しますか

Kappa: Your family is planning to visit your least favourite uncle tomorrow. You want to avoid him but you need a good excuse. Phone Tengu and issue an invitation to any of the activities in the table below. You must phrase your invitations as questions.

For example: あした、いっしょに コンサートを ききに いきませんか。

If Tengu doesn't agree, try another invitation. If you cannot find an activity that you both want to do, you have to visit that uncle!

Tengu: You have a date tomorrow that is very important to you. There is only one activity in the following table for which you would break your date. Decide which one it is and write down the appropriate number in your notebook. Reply to Kappa's invitations.

For example: **Refusing** すみません。コンサートは ききに いきたくないです。
Accepting ええ、いっしょに コンサートを ききに いきましょう。

コンサートを ききに いきます 1	こうえんへ バーベキューを しに いきます 2	やまへ スキーに いきます 3
とうきょう デパートで かいものを します 4	うちで おんがくを ききます 5	うみへ およぎに いきます 6
ファミコンで あそびます 7	うちで ビデオを みます 8	スケートを しに いきます 9

part 3 • unit 7

3 きょうは いい てんきですね

(いい てんきですね。 / そうですね。)
(いやなてんきですね。 / そうですね。)

Map of Japan showing:
- Sapporo 2°C (snow)
- 4°C (cloudy)
- 15°C (sun/cloud) — Hiroshima
- 14°C (rain) — Okayama
- 18°C (sun) — Kagoshima
- 6°C (sun/cloud) — Sendai
- Niigata
- Wakayama
- Tōkyō 10°C (rain)
- 13°C (sun)

Weather symbols:
- はれ (sun)
- くもり (cloud)
- あめ (umbrella)
- ゆき (snow)
- はれのち くもり
- くもりのち あめ
- きおん ℃: ど

Work in pairs and take turns.

Kappa: You are a weather forecaster. Choose four cities and report tomorrow's weather for each city, including the temperature.

Tengu: Listen carefully to find out the weather and temperature in the city Kappa is talking about.

For example:
かっぱ: あしたの てんきは はれでしょう。きおんは 十八どでしょう。
てんぐ: それは かごしまです。

Notes:
1. When talking about something that you are not sure of, such as the weather, use でしょう instead of です。
2. 0°C is れいど; 4°C is よんど; 7°C is ななど。

104　　　mirai 2

4 Weather forecast

You are going on holiday tomorrow. It is raining today so you are worried what the weather will be like. Listen to the weather forecast and fill in the weather conditions and the temperatures in the chart in English.

City	Weather	Temperature (°C)
ブリスベン		
シドニー		
メルボルン		
ホバート		
アデレード		
パース		
ダーウィン		
キャンベラ		

5 パズル

Complete the following note using vocabulary from the word list.

ゆかりさん、おげんきですか。こちらは せんしゅう、とても ＿＿＿＿ てんき でした。まいにち ＿＿＿ が ふりました。それに ＿＿＿＿＿＿ です。7＿ でした。きょうは ＿＿＿ です。いい ＿＿＿＿ です。やまには ＿＿＿ が たくさん ＿＿＿＿＿＿。だから ぼくは スキーに ＿＿＿＿＿ です。あしたも いい てんき ＿＿＿＿＿。だから、いっしょに ＿＿＿＿ に いきませんか。でんわして ＿＿＿＿＿。なおこ

Word list
はれ　　あめ　　　　ふりました　　いきたい　　てんき　　さむかった
いやな　　ください　　ゆき　　　　　スキー　　　ど　　　　でしょう

6 Missing particles

Complete the sentences by putting in one of the following particles.
Put a cross if you don't think any particle is necessary.

で、から、まで、を、が、に

a らいしゅう ＿＿＿＿ まち ＿＿＿＿ ロックコンサートが あります。

　しんぶん ＿＿＿＿ みました。六じ ＿＿＿＿ 八じ ＿＿＿＿ です。

b あした ＿＿＿＿ えいがスターが オーストラリア ＿＿＿＿ きます。

　ラジオ ＿＿＿＿ ききました。わたしは そのスター ＿＿＿＿ みたいです。

part 3 • unit 7

日本からの Eメール

Email　accessing mailbox...

　こんにちは。おげんきですか。せんしゅう、ぼくの クラスは くらしきへ えんそくに いきました。ぼくたちは でんしゃで いきました。とても いい てんきでした。たのしかったです。

　くらしきは とても ふるい まちです。それに、とても ゆうめいです。

　くらしきには はくぶつかんや じんじゃや てらが たくさん あります。ぼくたちは くらしきの ふるい いえと みせを 見に いきました。その ふるい たてものは ぜんぶ しろと くろです。かべは しろです。やねは くろです。とても きれいでした。それに、まちの 中に きれいな かわが あります。ぼくは しゃしんを たくさん とりました。かわの そばで おべんとうを たべました。ひる、きおんは 28どでした。だから、ぼくたちは みんな うみへ およぎに いきたかったです。でも、じかんが ありませんでした。かわりに、みせに おみやげを かいに いきました。
おへんじを まっています。
　　　　　　　　　　　　　　　　　　　　　　さようなら。
　　　　　　　　　　　　　　　　　　　　　　　しんご

くらしきがわ

Did you follow my description? Kurashiki is a very old town not far from the Inland Sea in Western Honshu. It has been a very prosperous town since the 16th century because it was a trading centre for rice and rush production — both very important commodities in Japan. The old part of the town has been preserved and, along the banks of the Kurashiki river, visitors can see the townhouses and storehouses of the wealthy merchants who lived there long ago. The houses have very distinctive architecture. The walls are whitewashed but with architectural details picked out in shiny black tiles, which also cover the roofs. The river is really pretty with old stone bridges and willow trees lining the banks.

This stone lantern, placed here in 1791, is all that remains of the many lanterns which used to light the paths beside the river.

There are several museums (はくぶつかん) housed in remodelled rice granaries. We particularly liked the Museum of Folkcraft, but had to spend most time in the Museum of Natural History because we were supposed to answer questions on the natural history of the Inland Sea. We also visited one of the temples (おてら), which is more than 1000 years old, and a shrine (じんじゃ). Many other high school groups were also visiting Kurashiki; the girls seemed to love the traditional toy shops and the craft shops.

By the way, girls often put お in front of places and some items. For example, a girl might say おてんき instead of just てんき. It makes their speech sound refined. If you are a girl and you don't use お where Japanese girls and women do, you might sound like one of the boys. If you are a boy you will sound rather like a girl if you use お in this way.

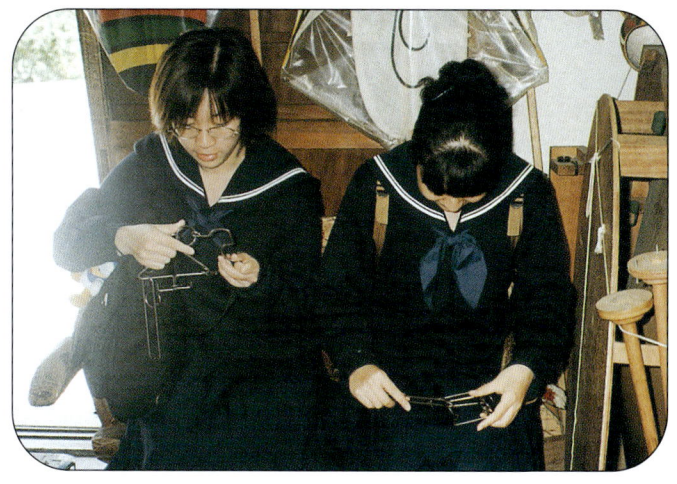

くらしきの ふるい いえは おもしろいですね。いまでも、人が その ふるい いえに すんで います。エアコンが 見えますか。

part 3 • unit 7

107

やった！

Asking where someone wants to go	どこ	へ	いき	たい	ですか。
Saying where you want to go	[Place]	へ／に	いき	たい	です。
Saying you don't want to go somewhere	[Place]	へ（は）	いき	たくない	です。
Asking if someone wants to do something	[Thing]	が／を	[verb] ~~ます~~	たい	ですか。
Saying you want to do something	[Thing]	が／を	[verb] ~~ます~~	たい	です。
Saying you don't want to do something	[Thing]	が／を	[verb] ~~ます~~	たくない	です。
Asking where someone obtained information	[Place]	で	見／きき／よみ	ました	か。
Saying where you obtained information	[Place]	で	見／きき／よみ	ました。	

Asking what the weather is like	てんきは	どう	ですか。
Answering: The weather is good/fine.	いい	てんき	です。
The weather is bad.	いやな	てんき	です。
It is fine/cloudy.	はれ／くもり	です。	
It is raining.	あめ	が	ふっています。
It is snowing.	ゆき	が	ふっています。
Saying what the weather will be like	はれ／あめ／くもり	でしょう。	

漢字　かんじ

One way of remembering

見　みます look at, see / みせます show 
— An eye on legs can *see* all around.

山　やま mountain / さん follows the name of a mountain, as in 富士山 (ふじさん) 
— This is easy to recognise as a simplified drawing of *mountains*.

カタカナ

シャ sha	シュ shu	シェ she	ショ sho
ジャ ja	ジュ ju	ジェ je	ジョ jo
シャンプー (shampoo) シャワー (shower) ジャム (jam)	パラシュート (parachute) バレーシューズ (ballet shoes) ジュース (juice)	シェパード (shepherd) シェーバー (shaver) ジェット (jet)	ショー (show) ショック (shock) ジョーカー (joker)
チャ cha	チュ chu	チェ che	チョ cho
チャイナタウン (Chinatown) チャレンジ (challenge) チャンス (chance)	チューインガム (chewing gum) チューバ (tuba) チューニング (tuning)	チェス (chess) チェッカー (checkers) チェックリスト (check list)	チョーク (chalk) チョコレート (chocolate) チョイス (choice)

part 3 • unit 7

カタカナ れんしゅう

1. Circle all the ski-related words.

アルパイン	ラケット	オリンピック	リフト	ボール
ピンポン	ブーツ	サングラス	スケート	アノラック
インストラクター	ジャンプ	テニス	クリケット	ヨット

2. Connect the pictured items with their names in katakana.

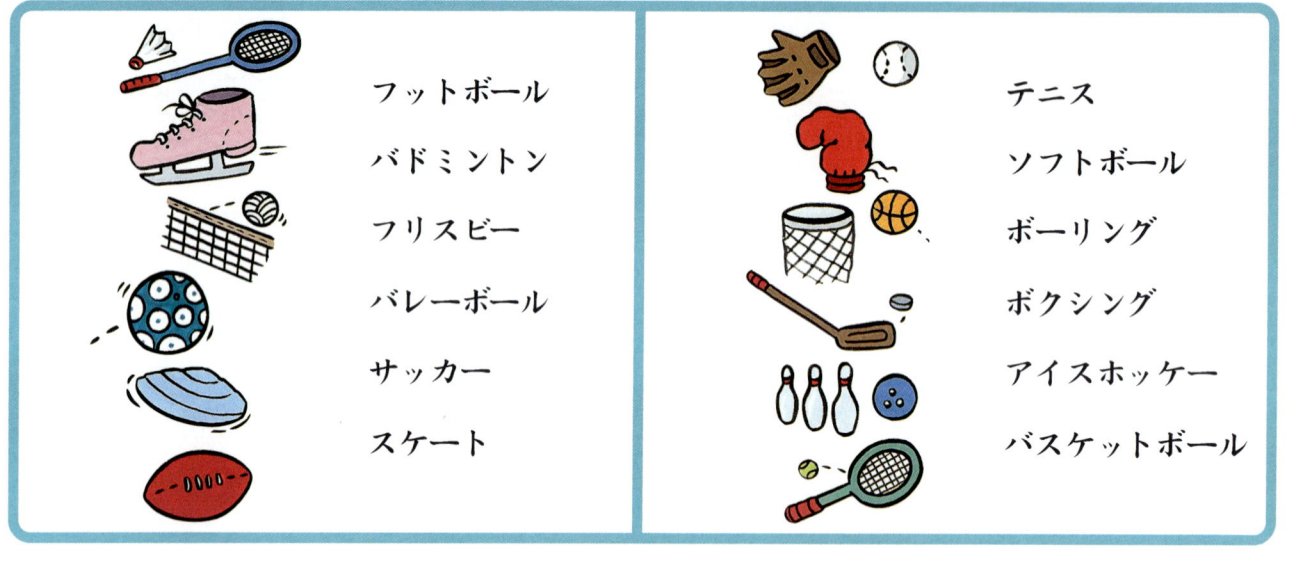

フットボール
バドミントン
フリスビー
バレーボール
サッカー
スケート

テニス
ソフトボール
ボーリング
ボクシング
アイスホッケー
バスケットボール

3. Find the following words in katakana and circle them.

chef
memo
pen
sharpener
shoot
napkin
chequebook
show
chocolate (choco)
private
chart
champion
tuning

ショ	ー	シャ	ー	プ	ナ	ー
チョ	コ	ジョ	チャ	ラ	プ	チュ
シュ	ー	ト	ン	イ	キ	ー
シェ	ペ	ギ	ピ	ベ	ン	ニ
フ	ン	ン	オ	ー	メ	ン
チャ	ー	ト	ン	ト	モ	グ
チェ	ッ	ク	ブ	ッ	ク	グ

The left-over katakana spell something good for your health: _____.

110   mirai 2

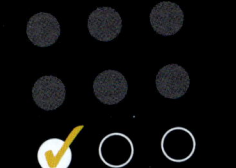

チェック しましょう！

Weather words

あめ	rain
(お)てんき	weather
きおん	temperature
くもり	cloudy
くもり のち あめ	cloudy; rain later
はれ	fine
はれ のち くもり	fine; cloudy later
ゆき	snow

Expressions

いいえ、ぜんぜん	not at all
うわあ！たすけて	Wow! Help!
かわりに	instead
きもちがいい	great feeling
ざんねんです	What a shame
それに	besides, moreover
はじめてです	the first time
わたしの ように	the way I am doing it

Time words

こんしゅう	this week
せんしゅう	last week
じかん	period of time
しゅうまつ	weekend
らいしゅう	next week
やすみ	holidays

Words related to buildings

いえ	house
かべ	walls
たてもの	building
やね	roof

Nouns

しんぶん	newspaper
スケート	skates, skating
スキー	ski, skiing
ファミコン	computer games

Suffixes

～ど	~ degrees centigrade

Places

(お)てら	temple
じんじゃ	shrine
はくぶつかん	museum

Adjective

さむい	cold

Verbs

みえます	can see

I can:
- ○ ask what someone wants to do
- ○ say what I want or wanted to do
- ○ talk about my weekend plans
- ○ say what I did and how it was
- ○ describe the weather
- ○ understand a weather forecast
- ○ say where I obtained information
- ○ read and write a description of an interesting place
- ○ read and write 山 and 見.

part 3 • unit 7

Unit 8

わさびは とても からい！

1. いらっしゃいませ。
   うわあ、おいしそうですねえ！

2. おなかが すきましたね。
   わたしは その おすしが 好きです。まぐろです。

3. その すしは なんですか。
   たまごです。やすいですよ。

4. おはしで たべましょうか。
   もちろん。

5. のどが かわきました。おちゃが ほしいですね。あの ウエーターは 日本人でしょうか。
   はい、日本人です。日本ごで ききましょう。

6
すみません！おちゃを 3つ ください。
はい、どうぞ。

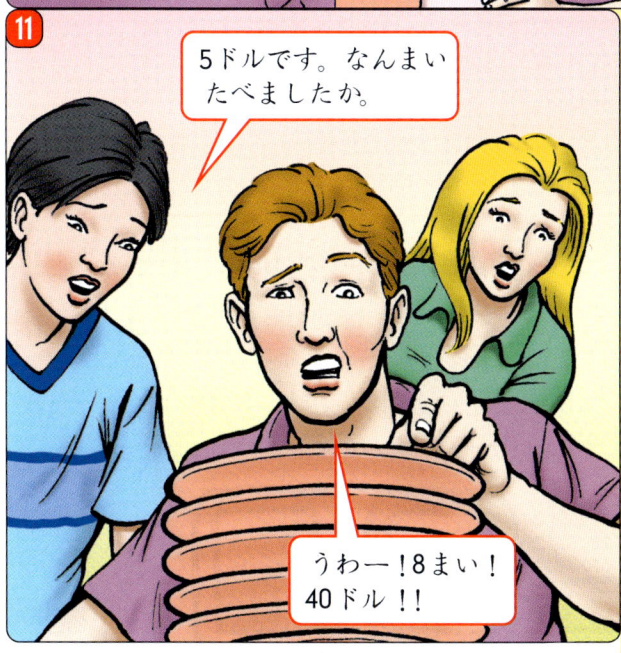

7
ぼくは みそしるを 1ぱい ください。
はい、どうぞ。
ありがとう。

8
これは なんですか。

9
わさびです。たべては だめです。

10
ケンくん、あかいのは たかいですよ。
いくらですか。

11
5ドルです。なんまい たべましたか。
うわー！8まい！40ドル！！

やってみよう
さがして ください

* a word that means *welcome*
* words that mean *I'm hungry*
* how to say *I want some tea*
* how to say *Three teas please*
* how to say *Let's speak in Japanese*
* how to say *One bowl of soup please*
* how to say *It looks delicious*
* how to say *The red ones are expensive*
* how to ask *How many plates?*
* how to say *I'm thirsty.*

あきのやまに ききましょう

Why does the waiter say いらっしゃいませ?

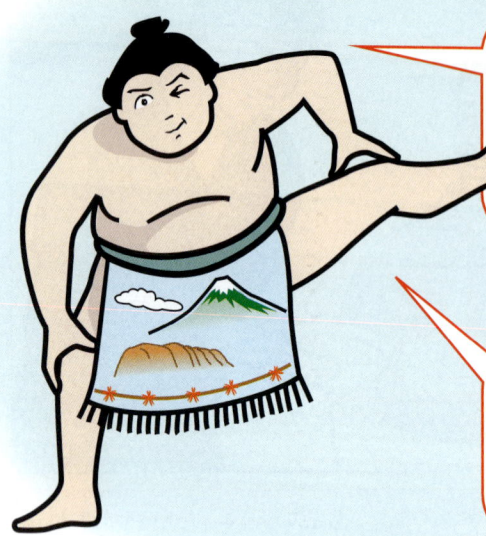

This the most common polite greeting to a customer in all restaurants, cafes and shops in Japan. It means welcome. It is related to the farewell on leaving home that you learned in *Mirai Stage 1*, いってらっしゃい, which means *Go and welcome back*.

If おいしそう means 'It looks delicious', can we add そう to other adjectives to mean 'It looks ...'?

Yes, you can replace the い of many い adjectives with そう. You can also add そう to some な adjectives, as in おじいさんは げんきそうです, which means *Grandpa looks fit*.

What does あかいのは mean?

This means *The red ones*. You can add の to many い adjectives to mean ~ *one* or ~ *ones*. You will find out more about this in Unit 9.

What are 3つ, 1ぱい and 8まい?

These are ways of counting various items. In English you would say, a bowl of soup, a slice of bread, a plate of scones, wouldn't you? Well, in Japanese we use counters for various items too, according to their shape. We count flat, thin things with the counter まい, bowls or cups with the counter はい and non-specific things with the counter つ. When ordering things in restaurants the つ counter is quite commonly used. Karen said みっつ when she ordered three teas. She could also have said おちゃを 3ばい ください (*Three cups of tea please*). There is a chart showing how to count using つ, はい and まい on page 116.

What's the difference between ～たいです and ほしいです?

They both mean 'want' but ～たいです means *want to do something*, as in おちゃが のみたいです and ほしいです means *want something*, as in おちゃが ほしいです。 The particle that goes before ほしいです is が. To say you *don't* want something, change ほしい to ほしくない. In this case, the particle changes to は. To find out more see page 117.

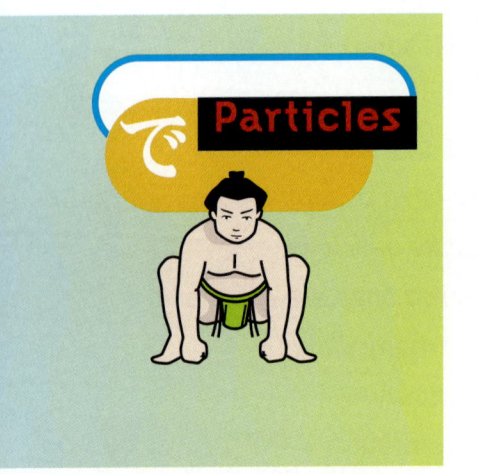

で Particles

You already know three uses of the particle で. In this unit you will discover another two. Again, で has the basic meaning of *using*. In the scene from the sushi bar, the two examples are:
おはしで たべましょう (let's eat *with* chopsticks) and
日本ごで ききましょう (Let's ask *in* Japanese).

Language / Implement — で — Verb

114　mirai 2

がんばれ

Saying how things look using そう

おいしそうです。
It looks delicious.

たのしそうです。
It looks enjoyable.

げんきそうです。
S/he looks fit.

Asking for a number of things using つ

おちゃを 1つ ください。
One tea please.

やきとりを 2つ ください。
Two yakitoris please.

パイを 3つ ください。
Three pies please.

Asking for a number of cups, bowls using はい

おちゃを 1ぱい ください。
One cup of tea please.

ごはんを 2はい ください。
Two bowls of rice please.

みそしるを 3ばい ください。
Three bowls of soup please.

Asking for a number of flat things using まい

おさらを 1まい ください。
One plate please.

カードを 2まい ください。
Two cards please.

かみを 3まい ください。
Three sheets of paper please.

Saying you want something

すしが ほしいです。
I want some sushi.

Saying you don't want something

ハンバーガーは ほしくないです。
I don't want a hamburger.

Asking someone to use a particular language/tool

日本ごで はなしましょう。
Let's speak in Japanese.

あかい えんぴつで かいて ください。
Please write with a red pencil.

part 3 • unit 8

ひとつ, いっぱい, いちまい

Counting things

Non-specific things (e.g. lollies, apples, stones)	Cups and bowls of things (e.g. tea, coffee, soup, rice, noodles)	Flat, thin things (e.g. plates, paper, shirts)
How many? いくつ？	なんばい？	なんまい？
1つ（ひとつ）	1ぱい（いっぱい）	1まい（いちまい）
2つ（ふたつ）	2はい（にはい）	2まい（にまい）
3つ（みっつ）	3ばい（さんばい）	3まい（さんまい）
4つ（よっつ）	4はい（よんはい）	4まい（よんまい）
5つ（いつつ）	5はい（ごはい）	5まい（ごまい）
6つ（むっつ）	6ぱい（ろっぱい）	6まい（ろくまい）
7つ（ななつ）	7はい（ななはい）	7まい（ななまい）
8つ（やっつ）	8はい／ぱい（はちはい／はっぱい）	8まい（はちまい）
9つ（ここのつ）	9はい（きゅうはい）	9まい（きゅうまい）
10（とお）	10ぱい（じゅっぱい）	10まい（じゅうまい）

Note: 1つ, 2つ and so on are also used to count ages as an alternative to ～さい.

Shopping trip

There are three shops here: Tsuko's shop, Haiko's shop and Maiko's shop. Look at the pictures below to see what each shop sells. Imagine you have to go to the shops and buy two items from each of them. You must decide how many of each item you would like to buy. Write your sentences in your notebook.

パイ　オレンジ　あめ	コーヒー　そば　スープ	さら　かみ　シャツ

Example: つ子さんの　みせ：パイを　3つ　ください。

おちゃが ほしいです／ほしくないです

Present tense		Past tense	
(want)	(don't want)	(wanted)	(didn't want)
ほしいです	ほしくないです	ほしかったです	ほしくなかったです

The sentence structure you should use is very simple, but notice the use of different particles for positive and negative statements.

- Thing/s you want + が ほしいです。
- Thing/s you wanted + が ほしかったです。
- Thing/s you don't want + は ほしくないです。
- Thing/s you didn't want + は ほしくなかったです。

1 Healthy eating

Imagine you are on a diet. Look at the pictures below and choose two things you want and two things you don't want. Write your sentences in your notebook.

ケーキ 　　　サンドイッチ 　　　オレンジ 　　　ホットドッグ

2 Lost in the bush!

Imagine you have just been rescued after being lost in the bush for a week! You are being interviewed by a TV reporter. Tell him/her what you were longing for while you were lost. You can use the picture in the bubbles for hints if you wish. Write your answers in the speech bubbles.

In Japanese you can't say what others want using 〜ほしいです. If you want to express what other people want, use 〜ほしいそうです。

For example:

ゆきさんは いぬが ほしいそうです。
やすくんは いぬは ほしくないそうです。

part 3 • unit 8

やってみよう

1 I want it / I don't want it

Work in pairs and take turns.

Tengu: Choose three pictures and comment to Kappa about each one using そうです and ほしいです. Use the appropriate counting word for each thing.

For example: このケーキは おいしそうですね。一つ ほしいです。

Kappa: Using the Amida kuji method follow the lines until you reach either a × or ○. If you reach a ○, agree with Tengu and say that you want it too. If you reach a ×, disagree with Tengu and say you don't want it.

For example: はい、おいしいですよ。ぼく／わたしも ほしいです。

　　　　　　or

　　　　　　いいえ、おいしくないですよ。ぼく／わたしは ほしくないです。

Note: To say something looks good, use よさそうです.

2 Listen in

In what situations will you hear these expressions? Listen carefully and write the correct numbers in the boxes.

- ○ is said when it is a nice day.
- ○ is said when you enter restaurants or shops.
- ○ is said when you are hungry.
- ○ is said when you are thirsty.
- ○ is said when you ask for a number of things in general.
- ○ is said when you ask for a number of bowls.
- ○ is said when you ask for a number of flat things.

3 Descriptions

Match the pictures with the appropriate description.

1 やさしくないです
2 おもしろくないです
3 やさしそうです
4 おもしろそうです
5 おいしそうです
6 やさしいです
7 おいしくないです
8 おもしろいです
9 おいしいです

4 Shopping with the judo club

You will hear the Mirai characters buying or ordering things at different places. Listen carefully and write what they order in the spaces provided.

a	Green tea		Yakitori	
b	Paper: 45 yen		90 yen	
c	Plates: red		blue	

d	Miso soup			
e	Eraser		Scissors	

5 Where to?

Your teacher's notice about a class excursion has blown into a puddle. You have been asked to rewrite it from what remains of the notice.

日本の レストランに いきましょう！

月よう　　　　いっしょに 日本の レストランに　　ましょう。レストランで おい　　りょうりを た　　しょう。みなさん、レストランで 日本　　はなして ください。えい　　はなしては　　です。それに、レストランで おは　　たべます。だから、れんしゅうして　　。

part 3 • unit 8　　119

日本からの Eメール

Email　accessing mailbox...

　こんにちは。おげんきですか。きょうは いやな てんきです。とても さむいです。きおんは 8どです。あめも ふっています。そとへ 行きたくないです。そちらの てんきは どうですか。

　ところで、きのう ともだちと そばを たべに 行きました。その そばやさんの なまえは「ごんだそば」です。えきの ちかくに あります。「ごんだそば」の メニューには いろいろな しゅるいの そばが あります。ともだちは てんぷらそばが 大好きです。だから、てんぷらそばを たべました。ぼくは やきとりと ざるそばの セットを たべました。この みせは たかくないです。ざるそばの セットは 600円です。そして、とても おいしいです。

　えきの ちかくに いろいろな みせが あります。「ごんだそば」の まえに ケーキやさんや すしやさんや マクドナルドが あります。この ケーキやさんの ケーキは おいしそうです。でも、ほんとうは おいしくないです。

I hope you understood most of this!

　Japan has a big population — more than 125 million people — and we all love eating out. There is a wide variety of restaurants wherever you happen to be. I live in a suburb, but nowhere is very far from shops and restaurants, so my friends, family and I often eat in the little restaurants nearby.

　The word や means shop, so (お)そばや means a noodle shop, from the word そば. We usually add さん as well to the kind of shop because we like to speak politely about the shops that serve our needs. These little restaurants and specialty shops are usually run by families.

　It is very easy to decide what you would like to eat in Japan because most of the cheaper restaurants have plastic replicas of their food in the windows and there are various kinds (いろいろな しゅるい) to choose from. The price is written alongside each dish. Dishes often come in sets. Each set usually includes soup, rice and pickled vegetables as well as the main dish.

てんぷらそばセット

120　mirai 2

When I go out with my friends, we like to eat hamburgers at McDonald's or pizza from a pizza parlour. We also love the sushi restaurants, which are called *kaitenzushi* because the food moves around. *Kaiten* means 'revolving'. The sushi chefs stand in the middle of a large circle making the sushi. There are many varieties of sushi, but they all have a base of cooked and vinegared rice. This is either formed into rice cakes with various kinds of raw fish placed on the top or made into a roll wrapped in *nori* (a sheet of processed seaweed). The centre of the roll contains fish and/or vegetables and pickles. The roll is sliced into sections like a swiss roll.

The price of the sushi depends on the cost of the fish used. The plates, colour-coded according to price, move along past diners on a little train or conveyor belt. The diners help themselves to the sushi they fancy and order drinks from waiters. When the diners have eaten their fill they call a waiter to add up the bill. The waiter counts the number of plates of different colours and works out the bill. Red plates might be ¥500, blue places might be ¥300 and so on. I have heard that there are sushi restaurants like this in many other countries now and that they are becoming very popular.

ぼくと ともだちは
かいてんずしが 大好きです。
いちばん おいしいのは
まぐろです。まぐろは ちょっと
たかいです。

ハンバーガーの みせも
たくさん あります。
ぼくは よく ともだちと
ハンバーガーを たべます。

日本の 大きい まちには いろいろな レストランが あります。
ちゅうごくりょうり、イタリアりょうり、タイりょうり、インドりょうり、アメリカりょうり、フランスりょうり、メキシコりょうりなどが あります。
どんな りょうりが 好きですか。
おしえて ください。

さようなら。

しんご

やった！

Saying how things look	[Thing] は	[adjective] い [adjective] な	そうです。
Asking for a number of things	[Thing] を	[quantity] (number + counter)	ください。
Counter for non-specific things Counter for bowls, cups, glasses Counter for flat, thin things	1つ 1ぱい 1まい	2つ 2はい 2まい	3つ 4つ… 3ばい 4はい… 3まい 4まい…
Saying you want something	[Thing]	が ほしい	です。
Saying you don't want something	[Thing]	は ほしくない	です。
Asking someone to use a particular language	[Language]	で [verb] て	ください。
Asking someone to use a particular tool	[Tool]	で [verb] て	ください。

漢字　かんじ

One way of remembering

行 — いきます / go — A crossroads is where you choose which way to *go*.

円 — えん / yen — Prices in Japan are always shown in *yen*.

カタカナ

ティ	ディ	デュ
ti	di	du
パーティー (party)	ディナー (dinner)	プロデューサー (producer)
スパゲッティ (spaghetti)	ディスコ (disco)	デューティーフリー (duty-free)
ティッシュペーパー (tissue paper)	ディンゴ (dingo)	デュエット (duet)

ニャ	ニュ	ヒュ	ビュ
nya	nyu	hyu	byu
ラザーニャ (lasagna)	ニュース (news)	ヒューストン (Houston)	**ピュ** pyu
ニャー、ニャー (miaow, miaow)	ニューヨーク (New York)	ヒューマン (human)	レビュー (review)
ターニャ (Tanya)	メニュー (menu)	ヒューマノイド (humanoid)	コンピューター (computer)

カタカナ れんしゅう

レストラン ニューヨーク

† サーロイン ステーキ	¥2,500
† ビーフ ハンバーガー	¥2,300
† ビーフ シチュー	¥2,000
† キング サーモン	¥3,200
† ロースト ポーク	¥2,500
† シーフード スパゲッティ	¥2,200
† ミックス グリル	¥2,800
† チキン サラダ	¥1,800
◇ コールド ビーフの オープン サンドイッチ	¥1,800
◇ ニューヨーク ステーキの サンドイッチ	¥1,800
◇ ハム チーズ サンドイッチ	¥1,000
☆ アメリカン ホット コーヒー	¥600
☆ ココア	¥500
☆ オレンジ ジュース	¥450
☆ アイス ティー	¥400
☆ アイス コーヒー	¥400

1 Looking for a main course

You are in a Japanese restaurant with your friends, Don and Cassy, but you are the only one who can read katakana! Don loves meat while Cassy and wants something light. Read the menu and tell them what their choices are. You like white meat. What will you decide to have?

What are Don's choices? _____

What are Cassy's choices? _____

What will you have? _____

2 Finding a drink

You would like to order something to drink too. Explain to your friends what choices the restaurant has. You and Don want a hot drink and Cassy wants a cold drink with no ice.

What are Don's choices? _____

What is Cassy's choice? _____

What will you drink? _____

チェック しましょう！

Counters

つ	general counter
まい	for flat things, (e.g. sheets)
はい	for bowls, cups, glasses

Countries

タイ	Thailand
インド	India
メキシコ	Mexico

Restaurants and shops

ウエイター	waiter
（お）すしや（さん）	sushi shop
（お）そばや（さん）	noodle shop
ケーキや（さん）	cake shop
セット	set
マクドナルド	McDonald's
メニュー	menu
レストラン	restaurant

Adjectives

やすい	cheap
たかい	expensive

Verbs

ききます	ask
おしえます	teach, tell

Expressions

あかいの	the red one
いらっしゃいませ	welcome
いろいろな しゅるい	various kinds
おいしそうです	It looks delicious
おなかが すきました	I'm hungry
ところで	by the way
のどが かわきました	I'm thirsty
もちろん	of course

Food and drink

あめ	lollies, candy
（お）ちゃ	green tea
（お）みそしる	miso soup
ざるそば	cold noodles served on a bamboo mat
たまご	egg
まぐろ	tuna
りょうり	dishes
わさび	Japanese horseradish

Currencies

円（えん）	yen
ドル	dollar

Place words

そと	outside
ちかくに	nearby

Things

（お）はし	chopsticks
（お）さら	plate
カード	card

I can:
- ○ count to 10 using the ひとつ system
- ○ count flat things
- ○ count cups or bowls
- ○ order food in a Japanese restaurant
- ○ say what I want
- ○ say what I don't want
- ○ ask someone to speak in English or in Japanese
- ○ ask someone to use a particular instrument
- ○ read and write about eating out.

part 3 • unit 8

Unit 9

あの あかい バッグは いくらですか

1.
- 十月一日に きょうとへ 父に あいに 行きます。
- ぼくも 九月に きょうとへ 行きます。ペンパルの みちこさんに あいに 行きます。

2.
- うわあ！わたしも きょうとに 行きたい！
- ぼくも きょうとに 行きたい！
- じゃ、いっしょに 行きましょう。父の うちに とまれますよ。

3.
- でも、ぼくは きょねん 日本へ いきました。それに、車を かいたいです。
- わたしは 父と母に ききます。日本は はじめてです。

4.
- ニッキーさんの へやです。
- きれいですね。なおみさんの お父さんは どこですか。

5.
- きょう、父は はたらいて います。あとで、あいに 行きましょう。まず、かいものに 行きましょう。

6.
- いらっしゃいませ！
- なにを かいたいですか。
- 母に きれいな シルクの バッグを かいたいです。
- じゃ、6かいの きものの うりばへ 行きましょう。

7

いらっしゃいませ！

あの あかい バッグは いくらですか。

あれは 一万円です。
いちまんえん

8

そうですか。もう すこし やすいのが ありますか。

この あおい バッグは 六千円です。
ろくせんえん

9

あの みどりのは いくらですか。

あ、あれは 三千円です。

じゃ、あれを ください。

かしこまりました。

10

いまから、父に あいに 行きましょう。

うずまさ えいがむら
Uzumasa MovieLand

11

ニッキーさんですね。はじめまして。

父です。

やってみよう

さがして ください

* words meaning *go to meet* or *go to see*
* the expression for *Pleased to meet you*
* the words for *How much?*
* the words meaning *sixth floor*
* the words for *Do you have a slightly cheaper one?*
* the expression for *Certainly madam/sir*
* the word for *first*
* the words for *Ask mum and dad*
* the words for *I want to buy . . . for mum.*

part 3 • unit 9

あきのやまに ききましょう

Why does Nikki say 父と 母に ききます? Doesn't ききます mean *hear* or *listen*?

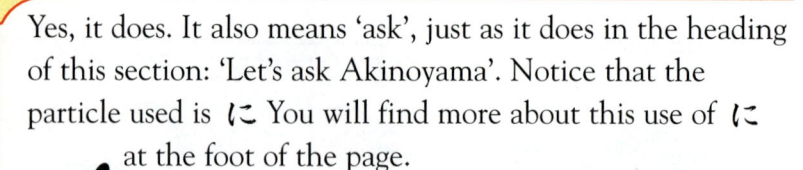

Yes, it does. It also means 'ask', just as it does in the heading of this section: 'Let's ask Akinoyama'. Notice that the particle used is に You will find more about this use of に at the foot of the page.

By the way, did you notice that あいに いきます means *go to see* in the sense of *go to meet someone*. In the same way, 見に いきます means *go to look at something*.

Why is the first day of the month ついたち?

The first day of the month has a special name: ついたち. The rest of the days as far as the 10th follow a similar counting system to the ふたつ, みっつ, よっつ system you have just learned. You will find all the days of the month spelt out on page 131. Just memorise 1–10, 14, 20 and 24. The rest of the days of the month are the numbers you already know plus にち.

Does 6かい mean the sixth floor?

Yes, it does. In Japan there is no word for the ground floor. The ground floor is called いっかい and so on.

What do いちまんえん and ろくせんえん mean?

いちまんえん means 10,000 yen and ろくせんえん means 6,000 yen. Japanese counting is quite simple. As you know, the word for 100 is ひゃく; there is no いち in front of it. But from 200 to 900 use the numbers for two to nine plus ひゃく. For example, にひゃく, さんびゃく and so on. One thousand is せん, also without いち, but 2000 is にせん and so on. Ten thousand is いちまん. This time いち *does* occur before まん. You will find a list of numbers from 100 to 100,000 on page 134.

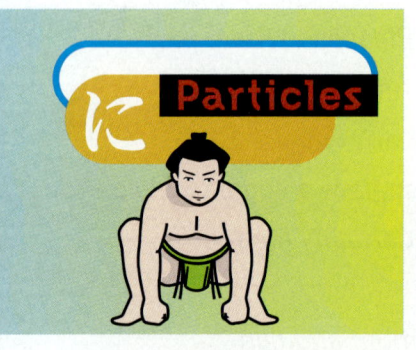

に Particles

In a sentence such as 母に バッグを かいたいです (*I want to buy a bag for my mother*) there are two particles, に and を. The を follows the direct object of the verb *buy* which is *bag*. The に follows the indirect object of the verb, *my mother*. Sometimes the sentence does not have a direct object, only an indirect object, as in 父と 母に ききます (*I will ask Mum and Dad*) and the title of this page, あきのやまに ききましょう.

Person verb (indirect object) → に

128   mirai 2

がんばれ

Asking what day of the month it is

きょうは なん日ですか。
(にち)

What day of the month is it today?

Answering

きょうは 一日です。
(ついたち)

Today is the first.

Asking what the date is

きょうは なん月 なん日ですか。
(がつ)(にち)

What is the date today?

Answering

きょうは 二月 二日です。
(にがつ ふつか)

Today is the second of February.

Asking how much something is

あの バッグは いくらですか。

How much is that bag?

Answering

6000円です。(ろくせん えんです。)

It is 6000 yen.

10,000円です。(いちまん えんです。)

It is 10,000 yen.

100ドルです。(ひゃく ドルです。)

It is 100 dollars.

Asking for a cheaper one

もう すこし やすいのが ありますか。

Do you have a slightly cheaper one?

Asking for a bigger one

もう すこし 大きいのが ありますか。

Do you have a slightly bigger one?

Asking for a smaller one

もう すこし 小さいのが ありますか。

Do you have a slightly smaller one?

Asking which floor something is on

きものの うりばは なんかいですか。

Answering

きもの うりばは 6かいです。

Saying you will ask someone

せんせいに ききます。

I will ask the teacher.

Saying you want to buy something for someone

母に プレゼントを かいたいです。

I want to buy a present for my mother.

part 3 • unit 9

なん月ですか

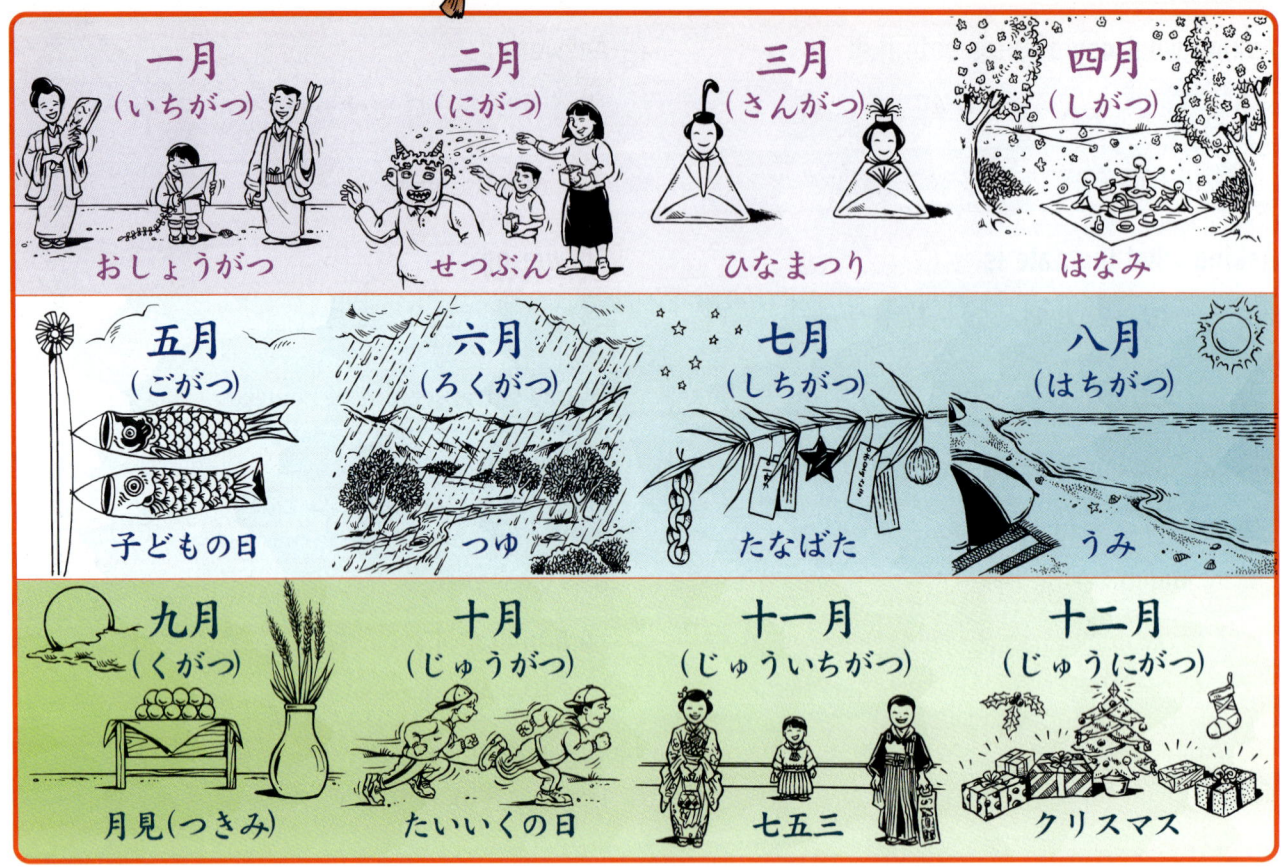

一月 (いちがつ) おしょうがつ	二月 (にがつ) せつぶん	三月 (さんがつ) ひなまつり	四月 (しがつ) はなみ
五月 (ごがつ) 子どもの日	六月 (ろくがつ) つゆ	七月 (しちがつ) たなばた	八月 (はちがつ) うみ
九月 (くがつ) 月見(つきみ)	十月 (じゅうがつ) たいいくの日	十一月 (じゅういちがつ) 七五三	十二月 (じゅうにがつ) クリスマス

1 Quiz

Study the calendar above and then answer the following questions.

a クリスマスは なん月ですか。
b はなみは なん月ですか。
c つゆは なん月ですか。
d 子どもの日は なん月ですか。
e おしょうがつは なん月ですか。
f せつぶんは なん月ですか。

2 Research

Find out as much as you can about the special days in Japan's calendar. Here are some very brief notes and questions to get you started.

おしょうがつ	New Year. What do people do? How long does it last?
せつぶん	A festival held in February. What do people do with beans and demon masks?
ひなまつり	The doll festival. What do girls do on this day?
はなみ	Cherry blossom viewing. What does it involve?
子どもの日	Children's day. What can be seen all over Japan on this day? What else happens?
つゆ	The rainy season. How long does it last? What is its other name?
たなばた	This festival is based on a legend. What was the legend? What do people do?
月見	Moon viewing can occur in either September or October; why?
たいいくの日	This is national sports day. What happens?
七五三	This is an important day for girls who are seven and three and boys who are five. What do they do?

130　　　mirai 2

なん日ですか

日よう日	月よう日	火よう日	水よう日	木よう日	金よう日	土よう日
	一日 ついたち	二日 ふつか	三日 みっか	四日 よっか	五日 いつか テスト	六日 むいか コンサート
七日 なのか	八日 ようか	九日 ここのか	十日 とおか	十一日 じゅういちにち	十二日 じゅうににち	十三日 じゅうさんにち
十四日 じゅうよっか	十五日 じゅうごにち	十六日 じゅうろくにち	十七日 じゅうなbelievingにち	十八日 じゅうはちにち	十九日 じゅうくにち	二十日 はつか ぶんかさい
二十一日 にじゅういちにち バーベキュー	二十二日 にじゅうににち	二十三日 にじゅうさんにち	二十四日 にじゅうよっか テスト	二十五日 にじゅうごにち	二十六日 にじゅうろくにち	二十七日 にじゅうななにち
二十八日 にじゅうはちにち	二十九日 にじゅうくにち	三十日 さんじゅうにち	三十一 さんじゅういちにち	You should learn how to say the first to the 10th by heart. Be careful with the dates in red! 14 is じゅうよっか; 20 is はつか; and 24 is にじゅうよっか.		

Look at the calendar above and answer the following questions.

a ぶんかさいは なん日ですか。
b コンサートは なん日ですか。
c テストは なん日ですか。
d バーベキューは なん日ですか。

Kappa and Tengu: Using the calendar above secretly fill in the dates of your own commitments: sports days, tests, piano lessons, family birthdays etc. Put a star against at least 12 days when you are free.

Tengu: You start. You would like Kappa to join you for the following activities.
  a A visit to a revolving sushi bar
  b Shopping in a department store
  c Watching a football match
  d Going to the beach

Negotiate days that you both are free. Organise at least three meetings.
Add the agreed dates to your calendar.

Kappa: Add the dates you have agreed to meet Tengu to your calendar.
You would like to invite Tengu to join you for the following activities.
  a A visit to an Italian restaurant
  b Going to see a movie
  c Swimming in the swimming pool
  d Fishing

Negotiate days that you both are free. Organise at least three meetings.
Add the agreed dates to your calendar.

For example:
てんぐ: かっぱさん、四日に えいがを 見に 行きましょうか。
かっぱ: 三日から 五日まで テストが あります。六日は どうですか。
てんぐ: はい、いいです。
かっぱ: じゃ、六日に 見に 行きましょう。

part 3 • unit 9

日本からの Eメール

Email accessing mailbox...

みなさん こんにちは。おげんきですか。こちらは はるです。せんしゅうから さくらの はなが さいて います。はなみの きせつです。

きのう、ぼくは かぞくと こうえんへ はなみに 行きました。そふと そぼも きました。母が 大きい おべんとうを つくりました。たくさんの 人が さくらの 木の 下で パーティーを して いました。カラオケも して いました。ぼくたちは カラオケを しませんでした。でも、とても たのしかったです。

あとで、ともだちと デパートへ 行きました。ぼくたちは 4かいが 一ばん 好きです。4かいには コンピューターの うりばと ゲームセンターが あります。だから、ぼくたちは いつも はじめに 4かいへ 行きます。5かいも おもしろいです。5かいは シーディーと 本の うりばです。8かいには いろいろな レストランが あります。ぼくたちの 一ばん 好きな みせは おこのみやきの みせです。よく このみせで ランチを たべます。でも、きのうは たべませんでした。かわりに、ゲームセンターで あそびました。ぼくは 1800円、ともだちは 2300円 つかいました。いま、おかねが ぜんぜん ありません。ゲームセンターは よくないですね。みなさんは ゲームセンターが 好きですか。

おこのみやき is a kind of thick pancake. You add your own choice of savoury topping, such as prawns or sliced pork, as it cooks. Each person cooks their own and then adds various sauces before eating. It is delicious.

What time do your department stores open? Ours open at 10 o'clock every morning and close at eight o'clock every evening. Outside the doors, one of the girls whose job it is to greet customers, waits until the exact stroke of 10. She then bows, opens the doors and lets the customers in. Inside, the store management stand in formal rows to welcome the customers, bowing all the time. All the assistants stand in front of their counters to bow to the first customers before returning to their places behind the counters. They all call out いらっしゃいませ!

In my favourite department store, they have girls dressed in cute dresses and hats standing by the lifts to welcome the customers into the lift. A similarly dressed girl stands inside the lift and calls out the floor and the kinds of merchandise for sale there. Beside the escalators, there used to be more girls bowing and saying いらっしゃいませ but these have been replaced with waxwork robots that look just like the girls with tapes inside saying いらっしゃいませ on a continuous loop!

Japan is a very long country, stretching from Hokkaido in the north — with its long, freezing winters — to subtropical Honshuu and tropical Okinawa in the south. Distinct seasons of three months are only really the case in central Honshuu.

> ところで、おおさかの きせつは はっきり しています。はるは 3月、4月、5月 です。なつは 6月、7月、8月です。あきは 9月、10月、11月です。ふゆは 12月、1月、2月です。ぼくの 好きな きせつは あきです。あきは スポーツや ぶんかさいの きせつです。あきは たいてい てんきが いいです。そらが きれいです。よるには 月が よく みえます。だから たくさんの人が 月見を します。

In Japan we have seven TV channels. My friends and I watch programs and films made in the USA and other countries such as Australia. There are also lots of programs made in Japan. The samurai movies are very popular and there is usually at least one showing every night. At Uzumasa Movieland in Kyoto they make some of these samurai movies. The whole village is a movie set so it is great fun to visit. You can often see ninja swinging along ropes high above your head and, if you are lucky, a samurai sword fight in and out of the houses or over the bridge. They also have an indoor studio, where you can sit and watch some of the scenes being shot. We had lunch there and took lots of photographs.

> せんしゅうは ぼくの たんじょうびでした。ともだちと うずまさ えいがむらへ 行きました。うずまさ えいがむらは きょうとに あります。そこで さむらい えいがを つくります。とても たのしかったです。しゃしんを たくさん とりました。おへんじを まって います。
> 　　　じゃ、また。　　　　　　　　　　　　　　しんご

デパートで

1 いくらですか — In Japan, most items are priced in 100s, 1000s and 10,000s of yen. Listen to these large numbers.

Phonetic changes:

	100	ひゃく
	200	にひゃく
b	300	さんびゃく
	400	よんひゃく
	500	ごひゃく
pp	600	ろっぴゃく
	700	ななひゃく
pp	800	はっぴゃく
	900	きゅうひゃく

	1,000	せん
	2,000	にせん
z	3,000	さんぜん
	4,000	よんせん
	5,000	ごせん
	6,000	ろくせん
	7,000	ななせん
ss	8,000	はっせん
	9,000	きゅうせん

10,000	いちまん
20,000	にまん
30,000	さんまん
40,000	よんまん
50,000	ごまん
60,000	ろくまん
70,000	ななまん
80,000	はちまん
90,000	きゅうまん
100,000	じゅうまん

Using the items below, act out a little skit between a shop assistant and a customer. Take turns.

For example:
てんぐ: いらっしゃいませ。
かっぱ: すみません、この　カメラは　いくらですか。
てんぐ: これは　3800円です。

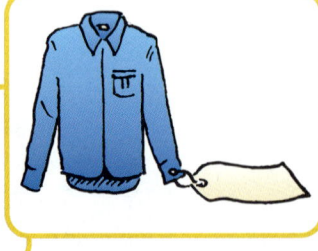

2 なんかいですか

Kappa: Using the department store guide, make up five true or false sentence giving the location of various items. Say this information to Tengu.

Tengu: Look at the chart and decide if Kappa is giving true or false information. If it is true say, ほんとうです。 If it is not true say, ほんとうじゃないです。

For example:
かっぱ: つくえの　うりばは　5かいです。
てんぐ: ほんとうじゃないです。

Rooftop	おくじょう	Pets
10	じゅっかい	Restaurants
9	きゅうかい	Books
8	はちかい	CDs
7	ななかい	Kimonos
6	ろっかい	Shoes
5	ごかい	TVs
4	よんかい	Desks
3	さんかい	Games
2	にかい	Computers
1	いっかい	Bags
Basement	ちか	Food

かいものを しましょう

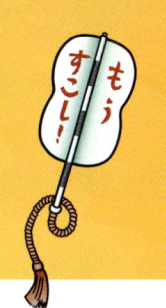

もうすこし！

Take turns with a partner and play the roles of the customer and shop assistant in each of these shops.

A: いらっしゃいませ。
B: あのう このケーキは なんの ケーキですか。
A: フルーツケーキです。
B: ひとつ いくらですか。
A: 250円です。
B: じゃ、それを 4つ ください。
A: はい、ぜんぶで 1000円です。

A: いらっしゃいませ。
B: あのう、あかい バッグは ありますか。
A: プレゼントですか。
B: はい、母に かいたいです。
A: そうですか。ええっと、これは どうですか。
B: きれいですね。これを ください。
A: はい、1800円です。

A: いらっしゃいませ。
B: これを 2つ ください。
A: はい、どうぞ。460円です。
B: じゃ、はい。
A: ありがとうございます。540円の おつりです。

A: いらっしゃいませ。
B: その みどりの T-シャツを みせて ください。
A: はい、どうぞ。
B: ちょっと 大きいです。もうすこし 小さいのが ありますか。
A: はい、これは どうですか。
B: ああ、ちょうど いいです。これに します。（これを ください。）
A: はい、3280円です。

A: いらっしゃいませ。
B: あのう、むらさきの いろえんぴつが ありますか。
A: すみません、むらさきのは いま ちょっと…
B: そうですか。じゃ、いいです。
A: どうも すみません。

やってみよう

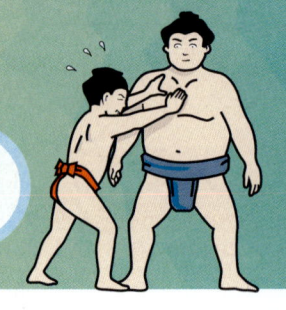

1 Present shopping

Ann is looking for Japanese souvenirs for her family. Listen to her conversation and complete the chart in English.

	For	Floor	Price
Sweater			
Sports shoes			
Silk tie			
Candy			

2 At your service!

Tengu: Make a list of the items pictured here in your notebook. Decide on which floor each item is sold and write that next to the item. Decide the price of each item and write that down too.

Kappa: Write four of the items pictured here in your notebook and decide the price you are prepared to pay.

Part 1

Tengu: You are working on the information counter of a department store. A Japanese tourist, Kappa, asks for help. Assist the customer in Japanese.

Kappa: You want to buy the items you have noted down. Find out on which floor they are sold.

For example:
かっぱ: あのう、すみません。
てんぐ: はい、いらっしゃいませ。
かっぱ: かばんの うりばは なんかいですか。
てんぐ: かばんの うりばは 4かいです。
かっぱ: ああ、そうですか。どうも。

Part 2

Tengu: Since you are the only member of staff who can speak Japanese, you are asked to help Kappa around the store. You have been authorised to offer a discount price if you wish!

Kappa: Ask Tengu the price of the items you want to buy. If the price is too high, ask for a cheaper one.

For example:
かっぱ: あのう、この かばんは いくらですか。
てんぐ: ええと、その かばんは 250ドルです。
かっぱ: そうですか。もう すこし やすいのは ありますか。
てんぐ: はい、あの かばんは 130ドルです。
かっぱ: じゃあ、あれを ください。
てんぐ: はい、かしこまりました。ありがとう ございます。

136　　　　　　　　　　mirai 2

やった！

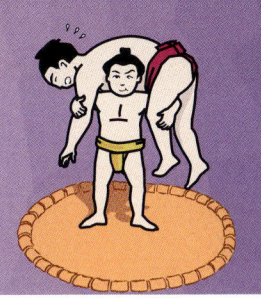

Asking what day of the month it is	きょう	は	なん日		ですか。
Saying the day of the month	きょう	は	[day of the month]		です。
Asking what the date is	きょう	は	なん月なん日		ですか。
Saying what the date is	きょう	は	[month/day of the month]		です。
Saying I will ask someone		[Person]	に	ききます。	
Saying I want to buy something for someone		[Person]	に	[object] を	かいたいです。
Asking how much something is		[Thing] は	いくら		ですか。
Saying how much something is			[Amount] えん		です。

Saying numbers up to 100,000

100s	1000s	10,000
ひゃく	せん	1 まん
2, 4, 5, 7, 9 ひゃく	2, 4–9 せん	100,000
3 びゃく	3 ぜん	10 まん
6, 8 ぴゃく		

Asking if there is a cheaper, bigger, smaller, more expensive one	もう すこし	[adjective]	の	が	ありますか。	
Asking which floor something is on	[Item]	の	うりば	は	なん	かい	ですか。
Saying what floor something is on	[Item]	の	うりば	は	[number]	かい	です。

漢字　かんじ

One way of remembering

車　くるま — car, cart
でんしゃ, じてんしゃ — train, bicycle

The chassis of a *car* from a mechanic's perspective.

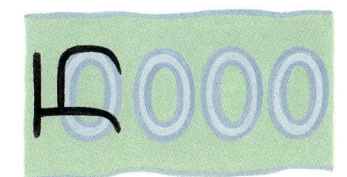

万　まん — 10,000

Turn the kanji on its side and you can *just* see a number 10 with a comma. The three zeros are missing.

part 3 • unit 9

カタカナ

ファ	フィ	フェ	フォ
fa	fi	fe	fo
ファックス fax ソファー sofa	フィンランド Finland フィットネス fitness	フェア プレー fair play カフェテリア cafeteria	カリフォルニア California フォード Ford

ミュ	リュ	ウェ	ウォ
myu	ryu	we	wo
ミュージカル musical エミュー emu	ボリューム volume ブリュッセル Brussels	ウェリントン Wellington ハイ ウェー highway	ウォークマン Walkman ウォルナッツ walnut

ヴァ	ヴィ	ヴ	ヴェ	ヴォ
va	vi	vu	ve	vo
ハーヴァード Harvard リヴァプール Liverpool	デイヴィッド David ヴィクトリア Victoria	ラヴ レター love letter	ヴェトナム Vietnam	ヴォーグ Vogue ヴォルヴォ Volvo

138　mirai 2

カタカナ れんしゅう

Christmas shopping

Amanda went to buy some Christmas presents while she was in Japan for her family and friends in Australia. She took the advertisement below with her but is not very good at reading katakana words yet. Help her find some good presents by suggesting one item from each floor. Write your suggestions in katakana next to the descriptions Amanda has given.

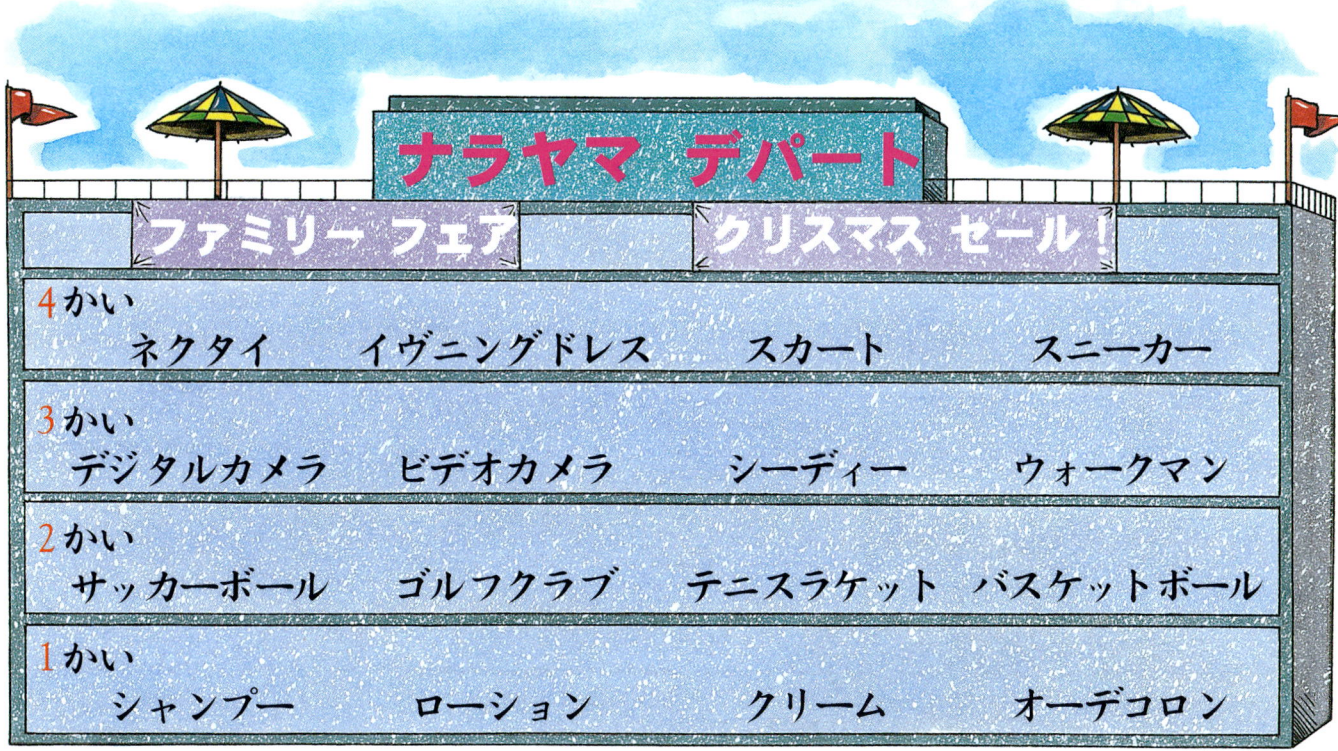

ナラヤマ デパート

ファミリー フェア　　　　クリスマス セール！

4かい
ネクタイ　　イヴニングドレス　　スカート　　スニーカー

3かい
デジタルカメラ　　ビデオカメラ　　シーディー　　ウォークマン

2かい
サッカーボール　　ゴルフクラブ　　テニスラケット　　バスケットボール

1かい
シャンプー　　ローション　　クリーム　　オーデコロン

1 First Floor

For her sister who is keen on her skin care:
_____

For her older brother who washes his hair every day: _____

2 Second Floor

For her mum who started taking tennis lessons: _____

For her dad who spends almost every weekend playing golf: _____

3 Third Floor

For her boyfriend who is into photography:
_____

For her girlfriend who loves listening to music:
_____

4 Fourth Floor

For her cousin who loves going out in the evenings dressed up: _____

For her younger brother who jogs every morning: _____

Amanda was wondering what the banners say. Can you tell her?

The banner on the left: _____

The banner on the right: _____

part 3 • unit 9

チェック しましょう！

AB pp. 98, 99

Verbs	
あいます	meet, see
ききます	ask
さいています	is blooming
さきます	bloom
しませんでした	did not do
たべませんでした	did not eat
つかいます	use, spend
つくります	make
とれます	can stay

Greeting	
はじめまして	Pleased to meet you

Other nouns			
おこのみやき	savoury pancake	そら	sky
カラオケ	karaoke	シーディー	CD
コンピューター	computer	きもの	kimono
さくらのき(木)	cherry tree	ほん(本)	book
シルクの バッグ	silk bag	ペンパル	penpal

Shopping			
いくらですか	How much?	かしこまりました	Certainly sir/madam
おつり	change	ちょうどいい	exactly right
うりば	counter	もう すこし	a slightly
おかね	money	やすいの	cheaper one

Counters	
〜かい	〜 floor
〜がつ(月)	〜 month
〜日	〜 day

Time words	
あとで	later
いつも	always
きょねん	last year
まず	first of all
いまから	from now
はじめに	firstly

Adjective	
まるい	round

Season words	
あき	autumn
おしょうがつ	New Year
きせつ	seasons
つきみ(月見)	moon viewing
つゆ	rainy season
なつ	summer
はなみ	cherry blossom viewing
はる	spring
ふゆ	winter

Places	
おくじょう	rooftop
ちか	basement
ゲームセンター	game centre
デパート	department store

Expression	
はっきりしています	are distinct

I can:
- ask what the date is
- say what the date is
- ask what floor/counter something is on
- ask the price of items
- understand prices given to me
- buy items
- say I will ask someone
- say I want to buy something for someone
- read and write a letter about shopping
- read and write 車 and 万.

mirai 2

part 4

ぶんかさい

Cultural festival

At the end of Part 4 you will be able to:

- write your friends' names in katakana
- follow instructions in Japanese to make an origami jumping frog
- sing some songs in Japanese
- follow directions in Japanese to cook some Japanese dishes
- follow instructions in Japanese to print kanji on a T-shirt
- take part in or understand a modern play in Japanese
- take part in or understand a play based on a traditional Japanese story.

Unit 10 なにを しましょうか

みなさん、8月2日は ぶんかさいですね。わたしたち、日本ごの クラスは なにを しましょうか。いろいろな かんがえを だしてください。

8月2日 ぶんかさいです

カエルの おりがみを つくりましょう。そして おりがみを 子どもたちに あげましょう。

おきゃくさんの なまえを カタカナで かきましょう。そして、その カードを おきゃくさんに あげましょう。

うたを うたいましょう。

日本の りょうりを つくりましょう。

げきを しましょう。

T-シャツに かんじを かきましょう。

すごいですね。がんばって！

カタカナで なまえを かきましょう
Names in katakana

女の子の なまえ

A
アリスン	Alison
アマンダ	Amanda
エイミー	Amy
アナ	Anna

B
ベッキー	Becky
ブランカ	Blanca
ブリタニー	Brittany
ブルック	Brooke

C
キャシー	Cathy
シャンテル	Chantelle
クレア	Claire
コートニー	Courtney

D
ダニエル	Danielle
デビー	Debbie
ダイアナ	Diana

E
エリザベス	Elizabeth
エミリー	Emily
エマ	Emma

FG
フィオナ	Fiona
ジョージア	Georgia
グレース	Grace

HI
ハナ	Hannah
ヘイリー	Hayley
ヘレン	Helen
イザベル	Isabel

JK
ジェイド	Jade
ジェニー	Jenny
ケイティー	Katie
カースティー	Kirsty

LM
リンダ	Linda
リサ	Lisa
マデリン	Madeline
メリサ	Melissa

NOP
ナタリー	Natalie
ニコラ	Nicola
オリヴィア	Olivia
ページ	Paige

R
レイチェル	Rachel
レベッカ	Rebecca
リネー	Renée
ローズマリー	Rosemary

S
サンドラ	Sandra
サラ	Sara/Sarah
ソフィー	Sophie/Sophy
ステファニー	Stephanie

T
ターニャ	Tanya
テリー	Terry
テリーザ	Theresa

UV
アスラ	Ursula
ヴァネッサ	Vanessa
ヴィクトリア	Victoria

WZ
ワンダ	Wanda
ウェンディー	Wendy
ゾーイ	Zoe

男の子の なまえ

A
アダム	Adam
エイドリアン	Adrian
エロン	Aaron
アンドリュー	Andrew

B
ベンジャミン	Benjamin
ブレット	Brett
ブレンダン	Brendan
ブラドリー	Bradley

C
キャメロン	Cameron
チャールズ	Charles
クリストファー	Christopher
クラーク	Clark

D
ダニエル	Daniel
デイヴィッド	David
ディラン	Dylan

E
エドモンド	Edmond
エドワード	Edward
イーサン	Ethan

FG
フランシス	Francis
ギャリー	Gary
グレン	Glen

H
ハーリー	Harley
ハリソン	Harrison
ハリー	Harry
ヘイデン	Hayden

IJ
イアン	Ian
ジェームス	James
ジョナサン	Jonathan
ジョシュア	Joshua

KL
キース	Keith
キーレン	Kieren
ローレンス	Laurence
ルーク	Luke

M
マーク	Mark
マシュー	Matthew
マイクル	Michael

N
ネイサン	Nathan
ニール	Neal/Neil
ニコラス	Nicholas

OP
オーエン	Owen
パトリック	Patrick
ポール	Paul

RS
ロバート	Robert
スコット	Scott
サイモン	Simon
スティーヴン	Steven

T
テリー	Terry
トーマス	Thomas
ティモシー	Timothy
トニー	Tony

VWZ
ヴィンセント	Vincent
ウェイン	Wayne
ウィリアム	William
ザカリー	Zachary

part 4 • unit 10

おりがみで かえるを つくりましょう！

ぴょんぴょん がえる (Jumping frog)

1 はんぶんに おります。

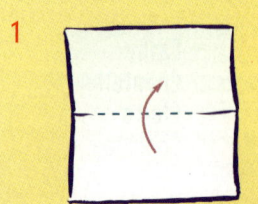

2 また、はんぶんに おります。

3 ひらきます。

4 Fold A across to D. Unfold.
さんかくに おります。そして、ひらきます。

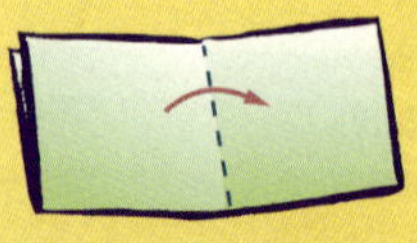

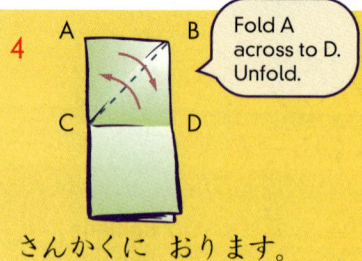

5 Fold B across to C. Unfold.
さんかくに おります。そして、ひらきます。

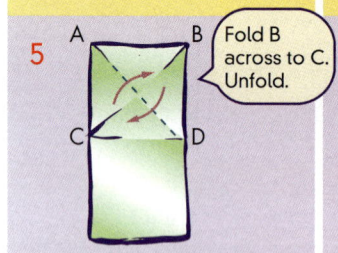

6 はんぶんに おります。

7 Form four double-layer triangles.
さんかくを つくります。

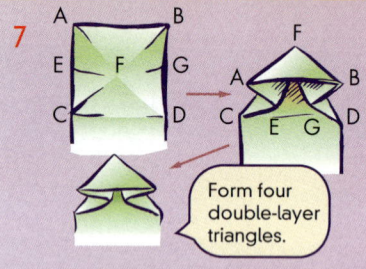

8 かえるの てを つくります。

9 したを はんぶんに おります。

10 ひだりと みぎを はんぶんに おります。

11 したを はんぶんに おります。

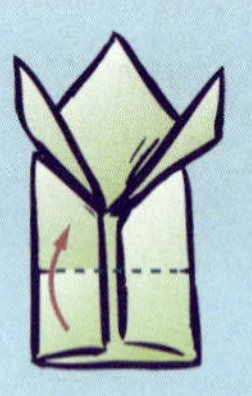

12 Fold A across to E. Fold B across to E. Unfold.
かどを さんかくに おります。

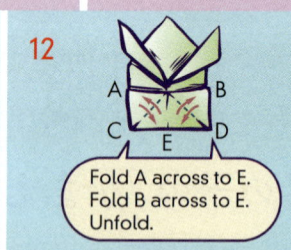

13 したに おろします。

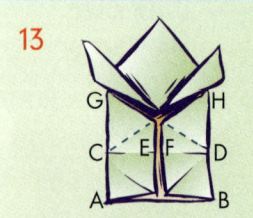

14 よこに ひらきます。

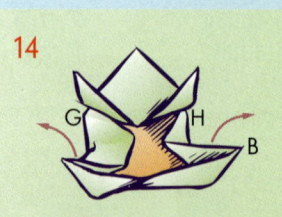

15 Make a little boat!

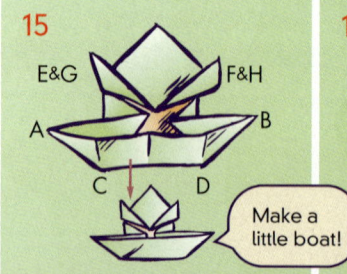

16  したに おろします。

17 かえるの あしを つくります。

18 はんぶんに おります。

19 また、はんぶんに おります。

20 できました！ Push with a finger and let it jump!

144　mirai 2

うたいましょう！

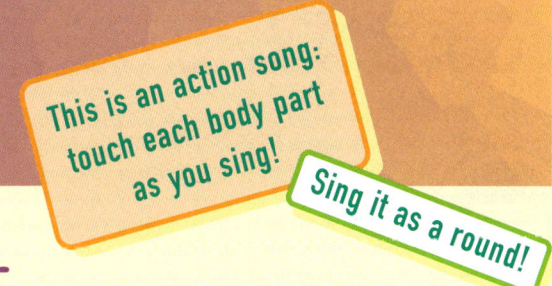

This is an action song: touch each body part as you sing!

Sing it as a round!

からだの うた

1　あし、うで、あたま。　　あし、うで、あたま。ゆび、ゆび、あしの　　ゆび。
2　くち、みみ、おなか。　　くち、みみ、おなか。めー、めー、てを　　　　たたこう。
3　のど、くび、せなか。　　のど、くび、せなか。はな、はな、ぶたの　　　はな。

日本のきせつ

1　はる は てんきが いいですよ　ララララ　はなみに 行きましょう

（男）　（女）　（男）　（女）
はなみが（はなみが）好きです（好きです）はなみに 行きましょう

2　なつは あつい日が つづきます
　　ララララ およぎに 行きましょう
　　うみが（うみが）好きです（好きです）
　　およぎに 行きましょう

3　あきは つきが きれいですよ
　　ララララ つきみに 行きましょう
　　つきが（つきが）好きです（好きです）
　　つきみに 行きましょう

4　ふゆは さむくて ゆきが ふる
　　ララララ スキーに 行きましょう
　　スキーが（スキーが）好きです（好きです）
　　スキーに 行きましょう

part 4 • unit 10

てまきずしで パーティーを しましょう！

おすしの ごはんを つくりましょう。　　**やさいや、さかなを きりましょう。**

1. おこめ（カップ 3ばい）を あらいます。
2. 水を カップ3ばい いれます。
3. 15ふん〜20ぷん
4. す 1/3 cup / しお 2 tsp / さとう 1 tbsp
5. ごはんに、まぜます。

1. たまごやきを つくります。それから、きります。
2. きゅうりや アボカドを きります。
3. まぐろを きります。
4. のりを きります。

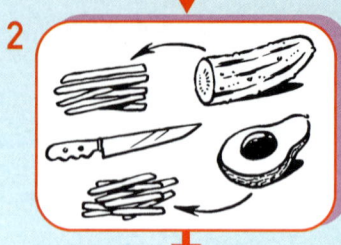

さあ、みんなで たべましょう。

いただきまーす！

しょうゆ　わさび

T-シャツ ペイント

T-シャツに かんじを かきましょう！

ようい しましょう

T-シャツ 1まい

ペイント セットと ブラシ （デパートで 7ドル ぐらい）

A4サイズ カードボードと かみ

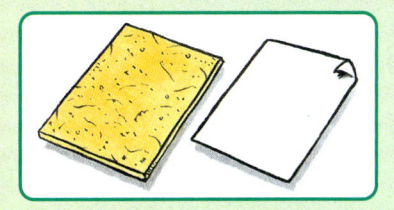

ピン 8つ

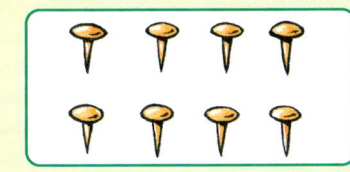

4B えんぴつ

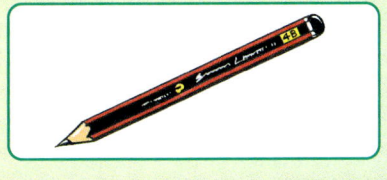

アイロン

T-シャツペイントの やりかた

1 カードボードを T-シャツの 中に いれます。

2 ピンで とめます。

3 4Bの えんぴつで かきます。

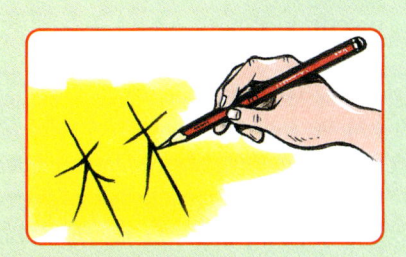

4 ペイントで 林を かきます。

5 かみを T-シャツの うえに おきます。

6 かみの 上を 5ふん アイロン します。

タジー そばは いちばん

Cast
- Mr/Ms Bond: marketing manager for Tasmanian products
- Mr/Ms Ukeda: Japanese buyer
- Akinoyama: a famous sumo wrestler
- Sobaya: maker and seller of cooked soba
- Japanese father
- Japanese mother
- Japanese boy
- Japanese girl
- Two cameramen
- Director

SCENE 1: Bond's office in Hobart

The curtain opens to reveal an office containing a desk with a chair on either side of it. There are coffee cups, a coffee maker, sugar bowl and milk jug on a tray on a small table. Bond is seated at the desk. The door opens and Ikeda enters. Bond jumps up to greet the visitor.

Bond: あっ、いけださん、おはようございます。
Ikeda: ボンドさん、おはようございます。ひさしぶりですね。
Bond: はい、ひさしぶりですね。とうきょうは さむいですか。
Ikeda: とても さむいです。タスマニアは いい てんきですね。
Bond: そうですね、なつは たいてい いい てんきです。でも、きのうは あめが ふりました。
Ikeda: ああ そうですか。
Bond: ええっと、コーヒーは いかがですか。
Ikeda: はい、おねがいします。
Bond pours out some coffee for the two of them. He passes the cup to Ikeda.
Bond: さとうと ミルクは？
Ikeda *(shaking head)*: いいえ、いりません。
Bond: じゃ、タスマニアの そばを みせても いいですか。*(He places a small packet of buckwheat kernels on the table.)* 日本人は そばが 大好きですね。タスマニアの そばは おいしいですよ。
Ikeda *(thinking)*: そうですね、でも、日本人は 日本の そばが 大好きです。ほかの くにの そばは あまり 好きじゃないです。ほかの くにの そばを あまり たべません。
Bond *(smiling and persuasive)*: じゃ、すばらしい こうこくを つくりましょう。ほんとうに タスマニアの そばは せかいで いちばんです。
Ikeda: こうこく？ いい アイディアですね。そうしましょう。
Bond *(looking at watch)*: あ、もう 12じはんですね。いっしょに ひるごはんを たべませんか。
Ikeda: ええ、いいですね。
They leave the office, the curtain closes.

SCENE 2: Film set in Japan

The curtain opens to reveal a film studio in Japan where a TV commercial is being shot. A soba shop is centre stage, the shop owner is behind the counter, a sumo wrestler wearing a yukata is seated with his back to the audience at the counter. There is a big pile of empty bowls on his right. There is also a wooden table and chairs a little to his right. Two cameramen are filming the action. A director is giving instructions. Ikeda is watching the making of the TV commercial.

Ikeda: じゃ、もういちど しましょう。はじめましょう。
Director: はい、はじめます。
He counts down using hand signals: 5, 4, 3, 2, 1.

Akinoyama: そばを もう 1ぱい ください。
Osobaya: はい、どうぞ。
He places a bowl of soba in front of Akinoyama who appears to eat it very quickly.
Akinoyama: もう 1ぱい ください。
Osobaya: はい、どうぞ。
He places another bowl of soba in front of Akinoyama who again eats it very quickly.
Akinoyama: もう 1ぱい ください。
Cameraman 1 moves the camera to focus on Osobaya behind the counter.
Osobaya (embarassed): すみません。あきのやまさんは このみせの 日本の おそばを ぜんぶ たべました。日本の おそばは もう ありません。でも、タスマニアの おそばは ありますよ。
Cameraman 2 focuses on Akinoyama who has turned sideways.
Akinoyama: タスマニアの おそば？ たべたくないです。おいしくないですよ。日本の そばが たべたいです。
Cameraman 1 moves back to film a family group of mum, dad and two children who enter the shop. They sit at the table.
Child 1: おそばが たべたい。
Child 2: ぼくも おそばが たべたい。
Father (to Osobaya): ええっと、そばを 4はい ください。
Osobaya: はい、どうぞ。
He quickly places four bowls of soba in front of the family.
Family: いただきます。
They start to eat slurping up the noodles.
Cameraman 2 moves the camera to film Akinoyama who is watching the family. He is licking his lips and holding his stomach.
Akinoyama: ああ、おなかが すきました。
Mother: わあ、この おそばは おいしいですね。
Child 1: とても おいしいですね。
Child 2: お父さん、もう 1ぱい ください。
Father: ほんとうに おいしいですね。みんな もう 1ぱい ほしいですか。
Everyone: はい。
Father to Osobaya: そばを もう 4はい ください。
Osobaya: はい、どうぞ。 (*He bring the four bowls to the family.*) この おそばは タスマニアの おそばです。
Father (surprised): ほんとうに、タスマニアの そばですか。とても おいしいですよ。
Akinoyama: ええっと、そばやさん、もう 1ぱい ください。
Osobaya: はい、どうぞ。
He places another bowl in front of Akinoyama.
Cameraman 1 moves the camera to film Akinoyama from behind the counter.
Akinoyama suspiciously takes a small taste, then starts sucking up noodles, faster and faster.
Akinoyama: うわ！ほんとうに おいしいです。もう 1ぱい ください。
Akinoyama (turning to smile at family): タジー そばは いちばん。
Director: カット。
Ikeda: できました。よかったです。ありがとう ございました。
Everyone gets up and starts to chat.

Curtain.

Ikeda enters from the front of stage right, holding a mobile phone.
Ikeda: もしもし。いけだです。ボンドさん いらっしゃいますか。ああ、ボンドさん こんにちは。はい、すもうの こうこくは よかったです。日本人は タジー そばが 大好きです。日本では いま タジー そばが すごい にんきです。ぼくは タスマニアの そばは ぜんぶ かいたいです。ありがとう ございました。じゃ、また らいげつ あいましょう。さようなら。
Exits left.

ももたろう

Peach Boy

キャスト

ナレーター
おじいさん
おばあさん
ももたろう
じんべい

いぬ
さる
とり
おにたち
こどもたち

SCENE 1: おじいさんと おばあさんの うち

Old man and old woman are sitting at a low table, having breakfast with chopsticks and rice bowls.

ナレーター： むかし むかし、小さい むらに おじいさんと おばあさんが すんでいました。おじいさんと おばあさんは 子どもが いませんでした。おじいさんは まいにち 山へ きを きりに 行きました。おばあさんは かわへ せんたくに 行きました。

おじいさん： ごちそうさま。じゃあ、山へ 行ってきます。

おばあさん： いってらっしゃい。

Old man carries a big basket off to the right.

おばあさん： わたしも かわへ せんたくに 行きましょう。

Old woman carries a laundry basket off to the right.

SCENE 2: かわ (Place a long blue cloth or paper across the stage.)

Old woman appears from the left with the basket. She kneels down, centre stage, at the edge of the river. She starts washing. A basketball-sized peach comes rolling down from the right towards the old woman.

おばあさん： あら？ 何でしょう？

Old woman reaches the peach and shakes off the water.

おばあさん： これは、これは、大きな もも！ うちに もって かえりましょう。おじいさんは ももが 大好きです。

Old woman carries the peach and the basket and walks off to the left.

SCENE 3 おじいさんと おばあさんの うち

Old woman sits at the low table, waiting for the old man. The knife and the peach are on the table. Old man appears from the right.

おじいさん: ただいま。

おばあさん *(happily dashing to the door)*: おかえりなさい。おじいさん、見て ください。大きい ももですよ。

おじいさん: わあ、大きいねえ。

Both come to the table. Old woman gives a knife to the old man.

おばあさん: おじいさん、これで きって ください。いっしょに たべましょう。

The peach splits in half and a baby boy is sitting inside.

おじいさん: わあ!! 何ですか。

Surprised, she drops the knife on the floor.

おばあさん: きゃあ!! *(Jumps backwards.)*

Both come nearer and have a closer look.

おじいさん: おとこの あかちゃんだ!

おばあさん: あかちゃん? まあ、ほんとう。かわいい。

ナレーター: おじいさんと おばあさんは この あかちゃんを ももたろうと よびました。

Old couple cuddle the baby happily.

SCENE 4: おじいさんと おばあさんの うち

ナレーター: ももたろうは まいにち ごはんを たくさん たべました。まいにち ジョギングを しました。まいにち けんどうの れんしゅうを しました。ももたろうは いま 十五さいです。もう 小さくないです。とても 大きいです。つよいです。

During the narration, Momotarō makes movements such as eating meals, jogging, practising kendo. He strikes a bodybuilder's pose.

   Momotaro, the old man and woman are eating at the low table, talking and laughing happily. Jinbei, an injured farmer appears from the left, falls on the ground in front of the door. The three of them hear the noise and look at each other in surprise.

おばあさん: あれ? 何ですか。

Momotaro rushes to the door and opens it. Old man follows him.

ももたろう: あっ! じんべいさんだ。だいじょうぶですか。

おじいさん: たいへんだ! じんべいさん!

Old man helps Jinbei from the ground and holds him in his arms.

じんべい *(panting from the pain)*: おにが きました! おにが きました! たすけて。

Old man and Momotaro look at each other. Old woman brings a towel for Jinbei and wipes his forehead. Freeze.

ナレーター: そのころ、その むらに ときどき おにが きました。おには わるい かいぶつです。*(One of the oni appears beside the narrator with an empty picture frame around his face. The narrator points to his face.)* そして、みんなの たべものや きものを とりました。子どもを いじめました。

Three or four farmers and children, one child carrying a lollypop, happily appear from the right and walk towards the oni. The oni *notices them and attacks them, takes the lollypop from the child and laughs in an evil manner.*

ももたろう: おじいさん、おばあさん。ぼくは いまから おにがしまへ 行きます。そして、おにを たいじします。

おじいさん: え? それは だめです。あぶないです。

おばあさん: 行っては だめです。おには とても こわいですよ。

ももたろう: だいじょうぶです。ぼくは 行きたいです。おには わるいです。だから、ぼくが やっつけます。 (Action of punching and beating up.)

おじいさん *(deep sigh)*: わかりました。ももたろう。行っても いいです。きをつけて。

おばあさん *(shocked)*: ああ、ももたろう。

ももたろう: おばあさん、ぼくは だいじょうぶです。(Takes old woman's hand.)

ナレーター: おばあさんは ももたろうに きびだんごを あげました。その きびだんごは 一ばん おいしいです。(Old woman brings a bag of dumplings and gives it to Momotarō.) おじいさんは はたを あげました。(Old man brings a flag and gives it to Momotarō.)

ももたろう: いってきます。

おじいさん: いってらっしゃい。

おばあさん: きをつけて。

Momotarō off to the right. Old man and woman wave for about five seconds to see him off. Old woman wipes tears with her sleeve.

SCENE 5: みちで (on the road to Onigashima)

Momotarō appears from the left. He looks tired.

ももたろう: ああ、あついなあ。みずが のみたいなあ。

Drinks some water from the water bottle. A dog appears from the left.

いぬ: ももたろうさん、どこへ 行きますか。

ももたろう: おにがしまへ 行きます。

いぬ: それは 何ですか。

Points at the bag of dumplings.

ももたろう: これは きびだんごです。おばあさんが つくりました。日本で 一ばん おいしいです。

いぬ: おなかが すきました。一つ ください。

ももたろう: はい、どうぞ。でも いっしょに きて ください。

Takes out one dumpling and gives it to the dog. Momotarō and the dog start walking. The dog is eating the dumpling. A monkey appears from the left.

さる: おいしそうですね。わたし/ぼくも 一つ ほしいです。

ももたろう: はい、どうぞ。でも、いっしょに きて ください。

Takes out one dumpling and give it to the monkey. Momotarō, the dog and the monkey start walking. The monkey is eating the dumpling. A bird appears from the left.

とり: 何を たべて いますか。わたし/ぼくも たべたいです。

ももたろう: はい、どうぞ。でも、いっしょに きて ください。

Takes out one dumpling and gives it to the bird.

SCENE 6 おにがしまで

Several oni are sitting in a circle drinking and eating happily.

ナレーター: ここは おにがしまです。おにの うちの まえです。おには うちの 中で
おさけを のんで います。とりは うちの 中を 見に 行きました。

The bird comes in from the left and flies around the oni's party, scouting.

さるが ドアを あけました。

The monkey comes in from the left, holding a key with a cheeky face and beckons to Momotarō and his party. Momotarō and his party come in from the left. Momotarō approaches the oni. The oni stop eating and look at him.

ももたろう: おい、おにたち！ みんなの たべものや きものを かえせ！

おに1: あっ、おとこの子だ！ *(Pointing at Momotarō.)* おいしそうだ！ たべましょう！
(Wipes his dribbling chin and approaches Momotarō.)

ももたろう: やあ。 *(Takes the sword out, runs to oni and fights him.)*

Oni cries out and falls onto the ground. Other oni stand up making angry noises and approach Momotarō. The bird pecks at some oni. The monkey scratches some oni's faces. The dog bites other oni. Momotarō keeps fighting yet more oni. After about 30 seconds of fighting, all oni are beaten. All oni kneel down and bow.

おに2: たすけて ください。

おに3: すみませんでした。

おに4: みんなの たべものや きものを かえします。

おに5: たからものも あげます。

いぬ、さる、とり: やった！！

Everyone jumps up and cheers. Momotarō holds up his flag and smiles. All oni carry boxes and give them to Momotarō.

ももたろう: ぼくたちは 日本一です。
いぬさん、さるさん、とりさん、ありがとう。

いぬ、さる、とり: どういたしまして、ももたろうさん。

ナレーター: ももたろうと いぬと さると とりは、うちに かえりました。
そして みんなに たからものを あげました。
めでたし、めでたし。

part 4 • unit 10

チェック しましょう！

おりがみ

おります	fold
おろします	bring down
かど	corner
さんかく	triangle
はんぶん	half
ひだり	left
ひらきます	open
みぎ	right
よこ	crosswise

てまきずし (sushi by hand)

あらいます	wash
いれます	put in
おこめ	uncooked rice
きゅうり	cucumber
さとう	sugar
しお	salt
しょうゆ	soy sauce
す	vinegar
たまごやき	plain omelette
まぜます	mix
やさい	vegetables

T-シャツ ペイント

おきます	place
とめます	fix, fasten
ピン	pin
やりかた	instructions
ようい します	prepare

日本の月

かさ	umbrella
けしき	scenery
なきます	call, croak
もっていきます	carry with you
もみじ	maple trees
ゆきぐに	snow country

ももたろう

あかちゃん	baby	たいじします	conquer
あぶない	dangerous	たからもの	treasure
いじめます	teases, bully	つよい	strong
(お)さけ	rice wine	ナレーター	narrator
おに	ogre, demon	はた	flag
おにがしま	ogre island	むら	village
かいぶつ	goblin	めでたし	happy ending
かえします	give back	もも	peach
かえせ	Give it back!	もってかえります	take home
きびだんご	millet dumpling	やっつけます	defeat
きります	cut	よびます	call, name
せんたく	washing	わるい	bad, evil

タジー そばは いちばん

いらっしゃいますか	is there? (polite)	おそば	buckwheat noodles
いります	require, need	にんき	popular
カット	cut	ひさしぶり	It's been a long time
こうこく	advertisement	ほか	other
すばらしい	wonderful	ミルク	milk

からだの うた

あしのゆび	toes
ぶた	pig

ぶんかさい

うた	song
おきゃくさん	guests, visitors
かんがえ	idea
げき	play
だします	present

I can:
- ○ follow directions to cook a Japanese meal
- ○ follow directions to make origami
- ○ follow directions to print kanji on a T-shirt
- ○ sing a song in Japanese
- ○ understand a play in Japanese.

154 mirai 2

Vocabulary list

English–Japanese

* Words marked with an asterisk are used on Katakana renshuu pages.

A

a slightly cheaper one	もう すこし やすいの
about, approximately	～くらい／ぐらい
accountant	かいけいし
after that, and	それから
alone, by myself	一人で（ひとりで）
a lot, many	たくさん
*Alpine	アルパイン
always	いつも
*America	アメリカ
and so on	など
animal hair	け
*anorak	アノラック
apartment	アパート
apple	りんご
arm	うで
ask	ききます
Australia	オーストラリア
autumn	あき
avocado	アボカド
awfully, very	とても

B

baby	あかちゃん
bad, evil	わるい
*badminton	バドミントン
bag	バッグ
*ball	ボール
bank	ぎんこう
*bartender	バーテンダー
baseball	やきゅう
basement	ちか
*basketball	バスケットボール
barbecue	バーベキュー
bathroom, bath	（お）ふろば、（お）ふろ
*beaver	ビーバー
bed	ベッド
*beef hamburger	ビーフ ハンバーガー
*beef stew	ビーフ シチュー
*beer	ビール
beside	そば
besides, moreover	それに
big, large	大きい（おおきい）
bigger	もっと 大きい
bird	とり
black	くろ
blond hair	きんぱつ
bloom	さきます
(is) blooming	さいて います
blue	あお
body	からだ
book	ほん
bookcase	ほんだな
*boots	ブーツ
*bowling	ボーリング
*boxing	ボクシング
boy	おとこの子
Brazil	ブラジル
bring down	おろします
brothers and sisters	きょうだい
buckwheat (noodles)	そば
Bugs Bunny	バッグスバニー
building	たてもの
by the way	ところで

C

cage	おり
cake shop	ケーキやさん
call, croak	なきます
call, name	よびます
call out	だします
*Canada	カナダ
can do	できます
cane toad	ひきがえる
can see	みえます
can stay	とまれます
can't do	できません
can't do much	あまり できません
carp-shaped kite	こいのぼり
carry with you	もって いきます

vocabulary 155

cast	キャスト	cow, bull, bullock	うし
cat	ねこ	*cream	クリーム
*CD	シーディー	*cricket	クリケット
cello	チェロ	crosswise	よこ
Certainly, sir/madam	かしこまりました	cucumber	きゅうり
*champion	チャンピオン	curly hair	カーリーヘア
change	おつり	curry	カレー
*chart	チャート	cut	きります、カット
cheap	やすい	cute	かわいい
*cheese sandwich	チーズサンドイッチ		
*chef	シェフ	**D**	
cherry blossom viewing	はなみ	dangerous	あぶない
cherry tree	さくらの き	~ day	～日
*chequebook	チェックブック	defeat	やっつけます
chest	むね	~ degrees	～ど
chest of drawers	たんす	delicious	おいしい
child	こども	*department store	デパート
children	こどもたち	did not do	しませんでした
*chicken salad	チキンサラダ	did not eat	たべませんでした
*chimpanzee	チンパンジー	*digital camera	デジタルカメラ
*chips	チップス	*dingo	ディンゴ
chocolate	チョコレート	dirty, messy	きたない
chopsticks	（お）はし	dishes, cooking	りょうり
*Christmas	クリスマス	dislike very much	だいきらいです
clean	そうじ します	*dog food	ドッグフード
clear	はっきり	does well	よく できます
clever	あたまがいい	don't know	わかりません
close to	ちかく（に）	don't know yet	まだ わかりません
cloudy	くもり	don't like	好(す)きじゃないです
club	クラブ	don't like (formal)	好(す)きでは ありません
cocoa	ココア	down, below	下(した)
coffee	コーヒー	dollar	ドル
cold	さむい	drinks	のみもの
comic	まんが		
company	かいしゃ	**E**	
*computer	コンピューター	ears	みみ
conquer	たいじします	eau de cologne	オーデコロン
cooler	クーラー	eggs	たまご
corner	かど	*emu	エミュー
counter (in a store)	うりば	(happy) ending	おわり、めでたし
counters for:		entrance hall	げんかん
bowls, cups	～はい	erupt	ふんかします
flat things, clothes	～まい	*evening dress	イヴニング ドレス
general things	～つ	every day	まいにち
small animals	～ひき	exactly right	ちょうど いい
countryside	いなか	expensive	たかい
		eyes	目(め)

F

face	かお
family	かぞく
fantastic, cool	かっこいい
far away	とおい
father	お父さん(おとうさん)
(my) father	父(ちち)
ferret	しろいたち
fine	はれ
first of all	まず
(the) first time	はじめてです
firstly	はじめに
fix, fasten	とめます
flag	はた
~ floor	～かい
flower bed	かだん
fly	はえ
fold	おります
foot and leg	あし
*football	フットボール
*France	フランス
freely	じゆうに
*frisbee	フリスビー
frog	かえる
from now	いまから
futon	ふとん

G

game centre	ゲームセンター
garden	にわ
gate	もん
girl	女の子(おんなのこ)
give	あげます
give back	かえします
Give it back!	かえせ！
go down	おります
go up, climb	のぼります
goat	やぎ
goblin	かいぶつ
*gold	ゴールド
*golf club	ゴルフ クラブ
good	いい
good idea	いい かんがえ
*gorilla	ゴリラ
(my) grandfather	そふ
(my) grandmother	そぼ
great feeling	きもちが いい
green	みどり(いろ)
green tea	おちゃ
grey/white hair	しらが
guest, visitor	おきゃくさん
guitar	ギター

H

hair	かみ
hairdresser	ヘアドレッサー
(in) half	はんぶん
*ham	ハム
hand	て
handicraft	しゅげい
happy ending	めでたし
hate, dislike	きらいです
have/has, there is/are	います
haven't, there isn't	いません
head	あたま
Help!	たすけて！
here, this place	こちら、ここ
hole	あな
*hot coffee	ホットコーヒー
hot spring	おんせん
house	いえ
Happy birthday	おたんじょうび おめでとう ございます
how many (animals)	なんびき
how many (people)	なんにん
how much	いくら
(I'm) hungry	おなかが すきました

I

*ice cream	アイスクリーム
*ice hockey	アイスホッケー
*iced coffee	アイスコーヒー
*iced tea	アイスティー
idea	かんがえ
I don't understand	わかりません
I'm hungry	おなかが すきました
I'm thirsty	のどが かわきました
in addition, besides	それに
in front	まえ
*India	インド
insect	むし
inside	中(なか)
instead	かわりに

vocabulary 157

instructions	やりかた	*Mexico	メキシコ
*instructor	インストラクター	millet dumpling	きびだんご
is there (very polite)	いらっしゃいます	*milk	ミルク
It looks delicious	おいしそうです	miso soup	(お)みそしる
I will introduce	しょうかいします	mix	まぜます
		*mixed grill	ミックスグリル
		monkey	さる

J

Japanese horseradish	わさび
Japanese-style room	わしつ
Just this for today	きょうは これで

*monorail	モノレール
moon viewing	月見（つきみ）
more	もっと
mosquito	か
mother	お母さん（おかあさん）
(my) mother	母（はは）
*motorbike	バイク
mouse, rat	ねずみ
Movie World	ムービーワールド
museum	はくぶつかん

K

*kangaroo	カンガルー
karaoke	カラオケ
*kettle	ケトル
kimono	きもの
kitchen	だいどころ
koala	コアラ
kookaburra	わらいかわせみ

N

*napkin	ナプキン
narrator	ナレーター
national park	こくりつこうえん
nearby	ちかく
newspaper	しんぶん
next week	らいしゅう
New Year	(お)しょうがつ
*New York	ニューヨーク
night, night time	よる
noodles on a bamboo plate	ざるそば
noodle shop	(お)そばやさん
nose	はな
Not at all	いいえ、ぜんぜん

L

last week	せんしゅう
last year	きょねん
later	あとで
(am, is, are) learning	ならって います
left	ひだり
*lemon	レモン
letter	てがみ
let's ride	のりましょう
library	としょかん
like	好きです（すきです）
living room	いま
(am, is, are) listening	きいて います
lollies, candy	あめ
*London	ロンドン
long	ながい
long ago, in the past	むかし
It's been a long time	ひさしぶりですね

O

Of course	もちろん
often	よく
ogre, demon	おに
Ogre Island	おにがしま
Oh!	あら！
old	ふるい
older brother	お兄さん（おにいさん）
(my) older brother	兄（あに）
older sister	おねえさん
(my) older sister	あね
Olympics	オリンピック
omelette	やきたまご

M

make	つくります
maple tree	もみじ
McDonald's	マクドナルド
*meat pie	ミートパイ
meet, see	あいます
*melon	メロン
*memo	メモ

158　　　　　　　　　　　　m i r a i 2

only child	ひとりっこ	rain	あめ
open	ひらきます	rainy season	つゆ
*open sandwich	オープン サンドイッチ	(am, is, are) reading	よんで います
orange	オレンジ（いろ）	red	あか
orange juice	オレンジジュース	red hair	あかげ
other	ほか	(the) red one	あかいの
outside	そと	ride	のります
		refrigerator	れいぞうこ
		required, need	いります
		restaurant	レストラン

P

*panda	パンダ	rice wine	（お）さけ
parachute	パラシュート	right	みぎ
part-time job	アルバイト	*roast pork	ローストポーク
peach	もも	rodeo	ロデオ
penpal	ペンパル	*Rome	ローマ
period of time	じかん	roof	やね
pet	ペット	rooftop	おくじょう
photo	しゃしん	room	へや
piano	ピアノ	round	まるい
pin	ピン	running	ランニング
pie	パイ		
pig	ぶた		

S

*pilot	パイロット	sad, poor	かわいそう（な）
*ping pong	ピンポン	salt	しお
pink	ピンク	*sandwich(es)	サンドイッチ
*pizza	ピザ	sausages	ソーセージ
place	おきます	savoury pancake(s)	おこのみやき
plain omelette	たまごやき	scary	こわい
play	げき	scenery	けしき
Pleased to meet you	はじめまして	*seafood spaghetti	シーフード スパゲッティ
poison	どく	seasons	きせつ
pond	いけ	(I can) see	みえます
popular	にんき	set	セット
(am, is, are) practising	れんしゅうして います	*shampoo	シャンプー
prepare	ようい します	*share	シェア
present	プレゼント	*sharpener	シャープナー
private	プライベート	sheep	ひつじ
*puma	ピューマ	shoe	くつ
purple	むらさき	shoe cupboard	くつばこ
put in	いれます	*shoot	シュート
		shop	みせ

Q

quiet	しずか（な）	shopping	かいもの
		short	みじかい

R

rabbit	うさぎ	shoulders	かた
*racket	ラケット	*shower	シャワー
radio	ラジオ	shrine	じんじゃ

vocabulary 159

silk bag	シルクの バッグ	take off, remove	ぬぎます
*sirloin steak	サーロインステーキ	(am, is, are) talking	はなして います
skate, skating	スケート	tease, bully	いじめます
ski, skiing	スキー	technology	ぎじゅつ
skilled, good at	じょうず(な)	temperature	きおん
*skirt	スカート	temple	(お)てら
sky	そら	*tennis	テニス
sliding screens	しょうじ	*Thailand	タイ
slippers	スリッパ	that (one) over there	あれ
small	小さい（ちいさい）	that ~ over there	あの～
snake	へび	that (one)	それ
*sneakers	スニーカー	that ~	その～
snow	ゆき	there is/are (inanimate)	あります
snow country	ゆきぐに	there is/are (animate)	います
snow house	かまくら	this (one)	これ
*soccer	サッカー	this ~	この～
sofa	ソファー	(I'm) thirsty	のどが かわきました
softball	ソフトボール	this week	こんしゅう
sometimes	ときどき	today	きょう
song	うた	toes	あしのゆび
soon	もうすぐ	together, the two of us	二人で（ふたりで）
South America	みなみ アメリカ	toilet	おてあらい（トイレ）
soy sauce	しょうゆ	tomato	トマト
*Spain	スペイン	tortoise	かめ
sport	スポーツ	treasure	たからもの
spring	はる	tree	き
*star	スター	triangle	さんかく
station	えき	tuna	まぐろ
stay, stop at	とまります	*tuning	チューニング
(can) stay	とまれます	TV	テレビ
stomach	おなか	*TV star	テレビスター
strange, odd	へん(な)		
strong	つよい	**U**	
stuntman	スタントマン	ugly	みにくい
sugar	さとう	umbrella	かさ
summer	なつ	uncooked rice	(お)こめ
*sunglasses	サングラス	university	だいがく
*supermarket	スーパー	unskilled, poor at	へた(な)
*surfing	サーフィン	up, above	上(うえ)
sushi shop	(お)すしやさん	use, spend	つかいます
*Switzerland	スイス		
		V	
T		various	いろいろ(な)
table	テーブル	various kinds	いろいろな しゅるい
tail	しっぽ	vegetables	やさい
take	とります	veranda	ベランダ

160　　　　　　　　　mirai 2

very	とても
*video	ビデオ
village	むら
vinegar	す
volcano	かざん
*volleyball	バレーボール

W

wait	まちます
waiter	ウエイター
*Walkman	ウォークマン
walls	かべ
washing	せんたく
(am, is, are) watching	みて います
wear (shoes, skirt, jeans)	はきます
wear (shirt, dress)	きます
weather	（お）てんき
weekend	しゅうまつ
Welcome	いらっしゃいませ
What kind of ~?	どんな～
What a shame	ざんねんです
Which ~?	どの～
Which one?	どれ
white	しろ
*wine	ワイン
winter	ふゆ
*wombat	ウォンバット
wonderful	すばらしい
work	しごと
(am, is, are) working	はたらいて います
woven, rush mat	たたみ
Wow!	うわあい！

Y

*yacht	ヨット
yellow	きいろ
yen	円（えん）
Yes, please	おねがいします
*yoghurt	ヨーグルト
(my) younger brother	おとうと
(my) younger sister	いもうと
your younger brother	おとうとさん
your younger sister	いもうとさん

Japanese—English

* Words marked with an asterisk are used on Katakana renshuu pages.

あ

*アイスクリーム	ice cream
*アイスティー	iced tea
*アイスホッケー	ice hockey
あいます	meet, see
あお	blue
あか	red
あかいの	the red one
あかげ	red hair
あかちゃん	baby
あき	autumn
あげます	give
あし	foot and leg
あしの ゆび	toes
あたま	head
あたまがいい	clever
あとで	later
あな	hole
あに (兄)	my older brother
アパート	apartment
あぶない	dangerous
あね	my older sister
あの〜	that ~ over there
*アノラック	anorak
アボカド	avocado
あまり できません	can't do much
あめ	lollies, candy
あめ	rain
*アメリカ	America
あら！	Oh!
あります	there is/are (inanimate)
アルバイト	part-time job
*アルパイン	Alpine
あれ	that (one) over there

い

いい	good
いい かんがえ	good idea
いいえ、ぜんぜん	Not at all
いえ	house
いくら	how much?
いけ	pond
いじめます	tease, bully
いつも	always
いなか	countryside
イヴニングドレス	evening dress
いま	living room
いまから	from now
います	have/has, there is/are (animate)
いません	haven't, there isn't
いもうと	my younger sister
いもうとさん	your younger sister
いらっしゃいます	is there (very polite)
いらっしゃいませ	Welcome
いります	required, need
いれます	put in
いろいろ(な)	various
いろいろな しゅるい	various kinds
*インストラクター	instructor
*インド	India

う

うえ (上)	up, above
ウエイター	waiter
*ウォークマン	Walkman
*ウォンバット	wombat
うさぎ	rabbit
うし	cow, bull
うた	song
うで	arm
うりば	counter
うわあい！	Wow!

え

えき	station
*エミュー	emu
えん (円)	yen

お

おいしかったです	was delicious
おいしそうです	looks delicious
オーストラリア	Australia
*オーデコロン	eau de cologne
*オープン サンドイッチ	open sandwich
おおきい (大きい)	large
おかあさん (お母さん)	mother
おきます	place

mirai 2

おきゃくさん	guest, visitor	かた	shoulders
おこのみやき	savoury pancake(s)	かだん	flower bed
おくじょう	rooftop	かっこいい	fantastic, cool
おたんじょうび おめでとう ございます	Happy birthday	かど	corner
		*カナダ	Canada
おちゃ	green tea	かべ	wall
おつり	change	かまくら	snow house
おてあらい（トイレ）	toilet	かみ	hair
おとうさん（お父さん）	father	かめ	tortoise
おとうと	my younger brother	からだ	body
おとうとさん	your younger brother	カレー	curry
おとこのこ(子)	boy	カラオケ	karaoke
おなか	stomach	かわいい	cute
おなかが すきました	I'm hungry	かわいそう（な）	sad, poor
おに	ogre, demon	かわりに	instead
おにいさん(お兄さん)	older brother	かんがえ	idea
おにがしま	Ogre Island	*カンガルー	kangaroo
おねえさん	older sister		
おねがいします	Yes, please	**き**	
おり	cage	き	tree
おります	fold	きいて います	(am, is, are) listening
おります	go down	きいろ	yellow
オリンピック	Olympics	きおん	temperature
オレンジ（いろ）	orange (colour)	きを つけて	take care
オレンジジュース	orange juice	ききます	ask
おろします	bring down	ききます	listen
おんせん	hot spring	ぎじゅつ	technology
おんなのこ（女の子）	girl	きせつ	seasons
		*ギター	guitar
か		きたない	dirty, messy
か	mosquito	きます	wear (shirt, dress)
～か、にち	~ day	きもちがいい	great feeling
カーリーヘア	curly hair	きもの	kimono
～かい	~ floor	きらいです	hate, dislike
かいけいし	accountant	きびだんご	millet dumpling
かいもの	shopping	きります	cut
かいしゃ	company	キャスト	cast
かいぶつ	goblin	きゅうり	cucumber
かえします	give back	きょう	today
かえせ！	Give it back!	きょうだい	brothers and sisters
かえる	frog	きょうは これで	Just this for today
かお	face	きょねん	last year
かさ	umbrella	ぎんこう	bank
かざん	volcano	きんぱつ	blond hair
かしこまりました	Certainly, sir/madam		
かぞく	family		

vocabulary 163

く

*クーラー	cooler
くつ	shoes
くつばこ	shoe cupboard
くもり	cloudy
～くらい／ぐらい	about, approximately
クラブ	club
*クリーム	cream
*クリケット	cricket
*クリスマス	Christmas
くろ	black

け

け	animal hair
ケーキやさん	cake shop
ゲームセンター	game centre
げき	play
けしき	scenery
*ケトル	kettle
げんかん	entry hall
げんき(な)	well, lively

こ

*コアラ	koala
こいのぼり	carp-shaped kite
*コーヒー	coffee
*コールドビーフ	cold beef
*ゴールド	gold
こくりつこうえん	national park
*ココア	cocoa
こちら、ここ	here, this place
こども	child/children
こどもたち	children
この～	this ~
(お)こめ	uncooked rice
*ゴリラ	gorilla
*ゴルフクラブ	golf club
これ	this (one)
こわい	scary
こんしゅう	this week
コンピューター	computer

さ

*サーフィン	surfing
*サーロイン ステーキ	sirloin steak
さいて います	is blooming
さきます	bloom
さくらの き	cherry tree
(お)さけ	rice wine
*サッカー	soccer
さとう	sugar
ざんねんです	What a shame
(お)そばやさん	noodle shop
さむい	cold
さる	monkey
ざるそば	noodles on a bamboo plate
さんかく	triangle
*サングラス	sunglasses
*サンドイッチ	sandwiches

し

*シーディー	CD
*シーフード スパゲッティ	seafood spaghetti
しお	salt
じかん	period of time
しごと	work
しずか(な)	quiet
した(下)	down, below
しっぽ	tail
しませんでした	did not do
*シャープナー	sharpener
しゃしん	photo
*シャワー	shower
*ジャンプ	jump
*シャンプー	shampoo
*シュート	shoot
しゅうまつ	weekend
じゆうに	freely
しゅげい	handicraft
*シェフ	chef
しょうかいします	(I will introduce)
(お)しょうがつ	New Year
しょうじ	sliding screens
じょうず(な)	skilled, good at
しょうゆ	soy sauce
シルクの バッグ	silk bag
しろ	white
しろいたち	ferret
じんじゃ	shrine
しんぶん	newspaper

す

す	vinegar
*スイス	Switzerland
*スーパー	supermarket
スポーツ	sport
*スカート	skirt
スキー	ski, skiing
すき(好き)じゃないです	don't like
すき(好き)では ありません	don't like (formal)
スケート	skate, skating
*スター	star
スタントマン	stuntman
*スニーカー	sneakers
すばらしい	wonderful
*スペイン	Spain
スリッパ	slippers

せ

セット	set
せんしゅう	last week
せんたく	washing

そ

そうじします	make clean
*ソーセージ	sausages
そと	outside
そば	buckwheat (noodles)
そば	beside
そふ	my grandfather
ソファー	sofa
*ソフトボール	softball
そぼ	my grandmother
そら	sky
それ	that (one)
それから	after that
それに	besides, moreover

た

*タイ	Thailand
だいがく	university
だいきらいです	dislike very much
たいじします	conquer
だいじょうぶ	It's okay
だいどころ	kitchen
たかい	expensive
たからもの	treasure
たくさん	a lot, many
だします	call out
たすけて！	Help!
たたみ	woven, rush mat
たてもの	building
たべませんでした	did not eat
たまご	eggs
たまごやき	plain omelette
たんす	chest of drawers

ち

ちいさい(小さい)	small
ちか	basement
*チーズ サンドイッチ	cheese sandwich
ちかく(に)	close to, nearby
*チキンサラダ	chicken salad
ちち(父)	my father
*チップス	chips
*チャート	chart
*チャンピオン	champion
*チューニング	tuning
*チェックブック	chequebook
チェロ	cello
ちょうどいい	exactly right
*チョコ	chocolate
*チンパンジー	chimpanzee

つ

～つ	counter for general things
つかいます	use, spend
つきみ(月見)	moon viewing
つくります	make
つゆ	rainy season
つよい	strong

て

*ディンゴ	dingo
テーブル	table
て	hand
てがみ	letter
できます	can do
できません	can't do
テニス	tennis
*デパート	department store
(お)てら	temple
テレビ	TV

*テレビスター	TV star
(お)てんき	weather

と

～ど	~ degrees
とおい	far away
ときどき	sometimes
どく	poison
ところで	by the way
としょかん	library
*ドッグフード	dog food
とても	awfully, very
どの～	which ~
トマト	tomato
とまります	stay, stop at
とまれます	can stay
とめます	fix, fasten
とり	bird
とります	take
ドル	dollar
どれ	which one
どんな～	what kind of ~

な

なか(中)	inside
ながい	long
なきます	call, croak
なつ	summer
など	and so on
ナプキン	napkin
ならって います	(am, is, are) learning
*ナレーター	narrator
なんにん	How many people?
なんびき	How many animals?

に

～にち、か(日)	~ day
*ニューヨーク	New York
にわ	garden
にんき	popular

ぬ

ぬいで ください	Please take off
ぬぎます	take off, remove

ね

ねこ	cat
ねずみ	mouse, rat

の

のどが かわきました	I'm thirsty
のぼります	go up, climb
のみもの	drinks
のりましょう	let's ride
のります	ride

は

*バーテンダー	bartender
バーベキュー	barbecue
パイ	pie
～はい	counter for bowls, cups
*バイク	motorbike
はいて ください	Please wear
*パイロット	pilot
はえ	fly
はきます	wear (on the feet)
バグスバニー	Bugs Bunny
はくぶつかん	museum
(お)はし	chopsticks
はじめまして	Pleased to meet you
はじめてです	the first time
はじめに	firstly
はっきり	clearly
バッグ	bag
*バドミントン	badminton
はな	nose
はなして います	(am, is, are) talking
はなみ	cherry blossom viewing
はは(母)	my mother
*ハム	ham
パラシュート	parachute
はる	spring
はれ	fine
*バレーボール	volleyball
*パンダ	panda
はんぶん	(in) half

ひ

ピアノ	piano
*ビーバー	beaver
*ビーフ シチュー	beef stew

166　　　　　　　　　　mirai 2

*ビーフ ハンバーガー	beef hamburger
*ビール	beer
～ひき	counter for small animals
ひきがえる	cane toad
*ピザ	pizza
ひさしぶりですね	It's been a long time
ひだり	left
ひつじ	sheep
*ビデオ	video
ひとりっこ	only child
ひとりで（一人で）	alone, by myself
*ピューマ	puma
ひらきます	open
ピンク（いろ）	pink
*ピンポン	ping pong

ふ

*ブーツ	boots
ぶた	pig
ふたりで（二人で）	together, the two of us
*フットボール	football
ふとん	futon
ふゆ	winter
*プライベート	private
*ブラジル	Brazil
*フランス	France
*フリスビー	frisbee
ふるい	old
プレゼント	present
（お）ふろ、（お）ふろば	bath, bathroom
ふんかします	erupt

へ

*ヘアドレッサー	hairdresser
へた（な）	unskilled, poor at
ペット	pet
ベッド	bed
へび	snake
へや	room
ベランダ	veranda
へん（な）	strange, odd
ペンパル	penpal

ほ

*ボーリング	bowling
*ボール	ball
ほか	other
*ボクシング	boxing
*ホット コーヒー	hot coffee
ほん	books
ほんだな	bookcase

ま

～まい	counter for flat things
まいにち	every day
まえ	in front
マクドナルド	McDonald's
まぐろ	tuna
まず	first of all
まぜます	mix
まだ わかりません	don't know yet
まちます	wait
まるい	round
まんが	comic

み

*ミートパイ	meat pie
みえます	can see
みぎ	right
みじかい	short
みせ	shop
（お）みそしる	miso soup
*ミックス グリル	mixed grill
みて います	(am, is, are) watching
みどり	green
みなみ アメリカ	South America
みにくい	ugly
みみ	ears
*ミルク	milk

む

ムービーワールド	Movie World
むかし	long ago, in the past
むし	insect
むね	chest
むら	village
むらさき	purple

め

め（目）	eyes
めでたし	happy ending
*メキシコ	Mexico
*メモ	memo
*メロン	melon

vocabulary 167

も

もうすぐ	soon
もうすこし やすいの	a slightly cheaper one
もちろん	of course
もって いきます	carry with you
もっと	more
もっと おおきい(大きい)	bigger
*モノレール	monorail
もみじ	maple tree
もも	peach
もん	gate

や

やぎ	goat
やきたまご	omelette
やさい	vegetables
やすい	cheap
やっつけます	defeat
やね	roof
やりかた	instructions

ゆ

ゆき	snow
ゆきぐに	snow country

よ

よういします	prepare
ようふく	clothes
*ヨーグルト	yoghurt
よく	often
よく できます	does well
よこ	crosswise
*ヨット	yacht
よびます	call, name
よる	night, night time
よんで います	(am, is, are) reading

ら

らいしゅう	next week
*ラケット	racket
ラジオ	radio
*ランニング	running

り

りょうり	dishes, cooking
りんご	apple

れ

れいぞうこ	refrigerator
レストラン	restaurant
*レモン	lemon
れんしゅうして います	(am, is, are) practising

ろ

*ロースト ポーク	roast pork
*ローマ	Rome
ロデオ	rodeo
*ロンドン	London

わ

*ワイン	wine
わかりません	don't know/understand
わさび	Japanese horseradish
わしつ	Japanese-style room
わらいかわせみ	kookaburra
わるい	bad, evil